English Grammar for Students of German

*The Study Guide
for Those Learning German*

Sixth Edition

Cecile Zorach
Franklin and Marshall College

Charlotte Melin
University of Minnesota

Adam Oberlin
Princeton University

The Olivia and Hill Press®

THE O&H STUDY GUIDES
Jacqueline Morton, editor

English Grammar for Students of Spanish
English Grammar for Students of French
English Grammar for Students of German
English Grammar for Students of Italian
English Grammar for Students of Latin
English Grammar for Students of Russian
English Grammar for Students of Japanese
English Grammar for Students of Arabic
English Grammar for Students of Chinese
Gramática española para estudiantes de inglés

Printed in the U.S.A.

ISBN: 978-0-934034-43-2

Library of Congress Control Number: 2014931224

CONTENTS

CONTENTS

WHAT DOES ENGLISH HAVE TO DO WITH GERMAN?

English Grammar for Students of German (EGSG) explains the grammatical terms that are in your textbook and shows how they
relate to English grammar. Once you understand how the terms
and concepts apply to English, it will be easier for you to understand and learn German grammar.

Each short chapter is divided into two sections, *In English* and
In German, both explain the same grammar point and alert you to
the similarities and differences between the two languages.

You will also find step-by-step tools to apply grammar rules and
to get from an English structure to a German structure. To help
you become a more efficient language learner, we offer specific
study tips for learning different types of words.

On our site, www.oliviahill.com, we help you customize *EGSG*
to popular 1st-year German college textbooks. Just go to *German
correlations,* click on the name of your textbook, and download
the pages to be read in *EGSG* before each lesson. To assess your
comprehension, you can download a *Review Booklet* and *Answer
Key* from our site.

Note: In keeping with our approach to introduce grammar from
the perspective of the language of today's students, our examples
are based on contemporary spoken English. The standard written
English equivalent is also given to facilitate the transition to
German.

TIPS FOR LEARNING GRAMMAR

Grammar is one of the tools you need to communicate orally and
in writing. Grammar rules are very useful because they enable a
speaker to move from the particular to the general. For instance,
the grammar rule to put an "s" when there is more than one
object (book vs. books) enables us to apply that to other words
(table vs. tables). Without rules, we'd be forced to memorize every
word separately.

1. Reading a grammar rule in your textbook is not sufficient.
   Make sure that you understand the explanation. Studying the
   examples to see how they illustrate the rule is as important as
   understanding the rule itself. If anything is not clear, be sure
   to ask the teacher at the first opportunity. Clear up problems
   as early as possible so that you don't fall behind.

2. As you progress in your studies, review previous lessons regularly. To facilitate learning, textbooks tend to focus on one grammar point per section. Bear in mind that these points are not independent; they are part of a whole. In other words, as you learn new rules, don't forget the ones you learned before.

3. Repetitive use of grammar rules in different contexts will help you understand how they are applied and how useful they are.

Tips for Learning Vocabulary

One aspect of language learning is remembering many foreign words.

To learn vocabulary — Flashcards are a good, handy tool for learning new words and their meaning. You can carry them with you, group them as you wish, and add information as you advance. Creating your own flashcards is an important first step in learning vocabulary.

1. Write the German word or expression on one side of an index card and its English equivalent on the other side.

2. On the German side add a short sentence using the word or expression. To make sure that your sentence is grammatically correct, copy an example from your textbook substituting the names of people and places with ones you know. It will be easier for you to remember a word in a familiar context. For review purposes, note down the page number of your textbook where the word is introduced.

3. On the German side include any irregularities and whatever information is relevant to the word in question. You will find specific suggestions under the *Study Tips* sections.

How to use the cards — Regardless of the side you're working on, always say the German word out loud.

1. Look at the German side first. Going from German to English is easier than from English to German because it only requires your recognizing the German word. Read the German word(s) out loud, giving the English equivalent, then check your answer on the English side.

2. When you go easily from German to English, turn the cards to the English side. Going from English to German is harder than going from German to English because you have to pull the word and its spelling out of your memory. Say the German

equivalent out loud as you write it down, then check the spelling. Some students prefer closing their eyes and visualizing the German word and its spelling.   80

3. As you progress, put aside the cards you know and concentrate on the ones you still don't know.

How to remember words — Below are suggestions to help you associate a German word with an English word with a similar meaning. This is the first step and it will put the German word in your short-term memory. Use and practice, the next step, will put the words in your long-term memory.

1. Sometimes words are easy to learn because they are similar in English and German. These words are easy to recognize in German, but you will have to concentrate on the differences in spelling and pronunciation.   90

address	Adresse
to swim	schwimmen
green	grün

2. Try to associate the German word with another German word that you already know.

Freund	freundlich	*friend, friendly*
abfahren	Abfahrt	*to depart, departure*
klein	verkleinern	*small, to reduce*

   100

3. If the German word has no similarities to English, rely on any association that is meaningful to you. Different types of associations work for different people. Find the one that works best for you. Here are some suggestions:

- Group words by topics — It is easier to learn new words if you group them according to themes such as food, clothing, sports, school, home, etc. Think about the different kinds of words you will need to communicate about a particular topic. Try to learn action and descriptive words along with the words for people, places, and things. For example, take the topic of your living situation. To create sentences, you need to know more than the words for furniture!   110

apartment	to rent	cheap, expensive
dorm	to live	clean, dirty
roommate	to share	friendly, nice

- Group words by topics — You may also find it helpful to group words by category, such as opposites (big ≠ small, tall ≠ short).

120 4. To reinforce the German word and its spelling, use it in a short sentence.

Tips for Learning Word Forms

Another aspect of language learning is remembering the various forms a word can take; for example, another form of *book* is *books* and *do* can take the form of *does* and *did*. As a general rule, the first part of the word indicates its meaning and the second part indicates its form.

To learn forms — Paper and pencil are the best tools to learn the
130 various forms of a word. You should write them down until you get them right. The following steps will make learning forms easier.

1. Look for a pattern in the different forms of a word.
   - Which letters, if any, remain constant?
   - Which letters change?
   - Is there a pattern to the changes?
   - Is this pattern the same as one you already know?
   - If this pattern is similar to one you already know, what are
140   the similarities and differences?

   We will help you establish patterns in the *Study Tips* following selected chapters.

2. Once you have established the pattern, it will be easy to memorize the forms.
   - Take a blank piece of paper and write down the forms while saying them out loud.
   - Continue until you are able to write all the forms correctly without referring to your textbook.

3. Write short sentences using the various forms.

150 **To review forms** — You can use flashcards to review forms, not to learn them. You will find suggestions on what to write on the cards under the *Study Tips*.

Tips for Effective Study

Before class — Study the sections in *EGSF* listed in the *German correlations* (see p. 1) that correspond to the assigned grammar topic. (If your textbook is not listed, refer to the detailed index for guidance.) You will learn the relevant grammatical terminology, the similarities and differences between English and
160 German, and how to avoid common pitfalls. Afterwards move on to your textbook. Take notes as you study; highlighting is not sufficient. The more often you write down and use vocabulary and

rules, the easier it will be for you to remember them. Good preparation enables you to take advantage of classroom activities.

In class — Take notes. This will remind you what the teacher considers important and will reinforce what you are studying. When your teacher gives you a new example or you hear a phrase while watching a video program, write it down so that you can analyze it. Once you have mastered a new concept, make up simple statements. Begin by modeling your sentences after the examples in your textbook. Later you will be able to express your own ideas.

Homework — Complete exercises and activities over several short periods of time rather than in one long session. Don't get behind. You need time to absorb the material and to develop the skills.

Written exercises — As you write German words or sentences, say them out loud. Each time you write, read, say and hear a word it reinforces it in your memory.

Objective — Your aim is to be able to communicate correctly in German, orally and in writing, without reference to a textbook or dictionary. The study tips throughout this handbook will help you with this learning process.

CHAPTER

1

WHAT'S IN A WORD?

When you learn a foreign language, in this case German, you must look at each word in four ways: MEANING, PART OF SPEECH, FUNCTION, and FORM.

MEANING

An English word may be connected to a German word that has a similar meaning.

Tree has the same meaning as the German word **Baum.**

Words with equivalent meanings are learned by memorizing vocabulary (see pp. 2-3). There are many words, called COGNATES, that have the same meaning and approximately the same spelling in English and German.

Haus	*house*
Garten	*garden*
Student	*student*
intelligent	*intelligent*

Occasionally knowing one German word will help you learn another.

Knowing that **Kellner** means *waiter* should help you learn that **Kellnerin** is *waitress*; or knowing that **wohnen** means *to live* and that **Zimmer** means *room* should help you learn that **Wohn-zimmer** means *living room.*

However, there is usually little similarity between words, and knowing one German word will not help you learn another. In general, you must memorize each vocabulary item separately.

Knowing that **Mann** means *man* will not help you learn that **Frau** means *woman.*

Words that have the same basic meaning in English and German rarely have identical meanings in all situations.

The word **Mann** generally has the same meaning as *man*, but it can also mean *husband*. The word **Frau** usually means *woman*, but it can also mean *wife*, a married woman, *Mrs.*, or even *Ms.*

In addition, every language has its own phrases or way of expressing ideas; these are called IDIOMATIC EXPRESSIONS or IDIOMS.

The expression *keep your fingers crossed* must be considered as a whole to be understood, not as individual words: *keep + fingers + crossed*. The equivalent German expression, **die**

Daumen drücken [word-for-word: press your thumbs], must also be considered as a whole.

You will have to be on the alert for these idioms because they cannot be translated word-for-word.   40

PART OF SPEECH

In English and German a word can be classified as belonging to one of eight categories called PARTS OF SPEECH.

noun	article
pronoun	adverb
verb	preposition
adjective	conjunction

Some parts of speech are further broken down according to type. Adjectives, for instance, can be descriptive, interrogative, demonstrative, or possessive. Each part of speech has its own rules for spelling, pronunciation, and use.   50

In order to choose the correct German equivalent of an English word, you must learn to identify its part of speech. For example, look at the word *plays* in the following sentences.

Axel *plays* soccer.
verb → **spielt**

Axel likes *plays*.
noun → **Schauspiele**   60

The English word is the same in both sentences. In German, however, different words are used, and different sets of rules apply, because each *plays* belongs to a different part of speech. The various sections of this handbook show you how to identify parts of speech so that you can choose the correct German words and the rules that apply to them.

FUNCTION

In English and German the role a word plays in a sentence is called its FUNCTION. Depending on the sentence, the same word can have a variety of functions.   70

     subject
     direct object
     indirect object
     object of a preposition

In order to choose the correct German equivalent of an English word, you must learn to identify its function. For example, look at the word *her* in the following sentences.

I don't know *her*.
direct object → **sie**   80

Have your told *her* your story?

indirect object └→ **ihr**

The English word is the same in both sentences. In German, however, different words are used, and different sets of rules apply, because each *her* has a different function. The various sections of this handbook show you how to identify the function of words so that you can choose the proper German words and the rules that apply to them.

FORM

In English and in German, a word can influence the form of another word, that is, its spelling and pronunciation. This "matching" is called **AGREEMENT** and it is said that one word "agrees" with another.

I am   *am* agrees with *I*
she is   *is* agrees with *she*

Agreement does not play a big role in English, but it is an important part of the German language. For example, look at the sentences below where the lines indicate which words must agree with one another.

*The blue **book** is on the big old table.*

Das blaue **Buch** ist auf dem großen alten **Tisch**.

In English, the only word that affects another word in the sentence is *book*, which causes us to say *is*. If the word were *books,* we would have to say *are*. In German, the word for *book* (**Buch**) not only affects the word for *is* (**ist**), but also the spelling and pronunciation of the German words for *the* (**das**) and *blue* (**blaue**). The words for *is on* (**ist auf**) and *table* (**Tisch**) affect the spelling and pronunciation of the equivalent words for *the* (**dem**), *big* (**großen**), and *old* (**alten**). The only word not affected by the words surrounding it is the word for *on* (**auf**).

As the various parts of speech are introduced in this handbook, we will go over "agreement" so that you learn which words agree with others and how the agreement is shown.

WHAT IS A NOUN?

A **NOUN** is a word that names a person, animal, place, thing, event, or idea. A noun that names a specific person, place, or thing, etc. is called a **PROPER NOUN**. A noun that does not name a specific person, place, or thing, etc. is called a **COMMON NOUN**.

> Ingrid is my friend.
> proper common
> noun   noun

- a person
  Jacob, Katie, Professor Meyer
  friend, sister, student, gardener, doctor
- an animal
  Snoopy, Fluffy, Mickey Mouse
  dog, falcon, fish, bear
- a place
  Zurich, Bavaria, New York, Austria, Europe
  stadium, restaurant, city, state, country
- a thing
  Monday, White House, Volkswagen
  desk, house, border, water, hand
- an event
  or activity
  the Olympics, Thanksgiving
  birth, graduation, jogging, growth
- an idea
  or concept
  truth, poverty, peace, fear, beauty
  time, humor, justice, hatred

As you can see, a noun is not only a word that names something that is tangible (i.e., something you can touch), such as *desk, restaurant,* or *White House,* it can also be the name of something that is abstract (i.e., that you cannot touch), such as *truth, peace,* and *humor.*

A noun made up of two or more words is called a **COMPOUND NOUN**. A compound noun may be made up of two common nouns written as one word *(snowball),* as two words *(school year),* or with a hyphen *(self-interest).* It can also be a combination of a common noun and other parts of speech such as *Civil War* and *Berlin Wall.*

IN ENGLISH

Proper nouns always begin with a capital letter. Common nouns, however, only begin with a capital letter when they are the first word of a sentence or question.

To help you learn to recognize nouns, look at the paragraph below where the nouns are in *italics.*

> The *United States* imports many *items* from German-speaking *countries*. German *automobiles*, ranging from moderately

1

10

20

30

priced *models* to elegant *cars*, have earned a *reputation* here
for their excellent *performance*. *Germany* also supplies us with
fine *tools, cameras,* and *electronics.* Many *Americans* value
watches imported from *Switzerland.* Nearly everyone in our
country appreciates the *taste* of Swiss *chocolate.*

IN GERMAN

Nouns are identified the same way as they are in English. In
German, however, they are very easy to recognize since all
nouns, proper and common, are capitalized, regardless of
where they are in a sentence.

TERMS USED TO TALK ABOUT NOUNS

- **Case** — In German, a noun can have a variety of forms
  depending on its function in the sentence (see *What is Meant by
  Case?*, p. 28).

- **Gender** — In German, a noun has a gender; that is, it can be
  classified according to whether it is masculine, feminine, or
  neuter (see *What is Meant by Gender?*, p. 18).

- **Number** — A noun has number; that is, it can be identified as
  being singular or plural (see *What is Meant by Number?*, p. 15).

- **Function** — A noun can have a variety of functions in a sentence; that is, it can be the subject of the sentence (see *What is
  a Subject?*, p. 40), a predicate noun (see *What is a Predicate
  Noun?*, p. 43), or an object (see *What is an Object?*, p. 55).

WHAT ARE PREFIXES AND SUFFIXES?

A **PREFIX** consists of one or more syllables added to the beginning of   1
a word to change that word's meaning.

nuclear	→	*anti*nuclear
approve	→	*dis*approve

A **SUFFIX** consists of one or more syllables added to the end of a
word to change that word into a different part of speech (see p. 7).

gentle (adjective)	→	gentle*ness* (noun)
love (noun)	→	lov*able* (adjective)

To see how prefixes and suffixes work, look at the various English   10
words that come from the Latin verb **duco** *(to lead)*. Different prefixes give us verbs such as *in*duce, *re*duce, *se*duce, *pro*duce, and
*intro*duce. Added suffixes result in different parts of speech, for
example: induc*tion* (noun), induc*tive* (adjective), induc*tively*
(adverb).

IN ENGLISH

Many English prefixes and suffixes come from Latin and Greek,
and some are of native Germanic origin. A good English dictionary will tell you the meaning and function of the various prefixes and suffixes.   20

Knowing English suffixes can help you identify the parts of
speech in a sentence and increase your English vocabulary.

-able, -ible	toler*able*	→ adjective
-ly	quick*ly*	→ adverb
-ence, -ance	reli*ance*	→ noun

NOUNS FORMED WITH SUFFIXES (see *What is a Noun?*, p. 9)

By adding a prefix to an existing noun, you can form a new
noun with a different meaning.

anti- + body (against)	→	*anti*body 30
sub- + marine (under)	→	*sub*marine
mal- + nutrition (bad)	→	*mal*nutrition

VERBS FORMED WITH PREFIXES (see *What is a Verb?*, p. 25)
A new verb with a different meaning can be formed by adding
a prefix to an existing verb.

He *used* the tool correctly.
    |
   verb

He *mis*used the tool, and it broke.
    |
   verb

A verb can also be formed by adding a prefix to another part of
speech.

Anja is my new *friend*.
      |
    noun

She *be*friended me on my first day at the new school.
     |
    verb

IN GERMAN

As in English, prefixes and suffixes can be used to change the
meaning of words and to change a word's part of speech.

NOUNS FORMED WITH SUFFIXES

Certain suffixes not only affect the meaning of a noun but also
determine the gender of the noun being formed (see *What is
Meant by Gender?*, p. 18).

- noun + **-chen** and **-lein** → new noun is neuter
  These suffixes show that the noun is a diminutive, i.e., something reduced in size.

NOUN		NEW NOUN NEUTER	
das Brot (neut.)	*bread*	das Bröt**chen**	*roll, little bread*
der Brief (masc.)	*letter*	das Brief**lein**	*small letter*
die Frau (fem.)	*woman*	das Fräu**lein**	*young woman*

- adjective + **-heit** and **-keit** → feminine noun
  These suffixes turn an adjective into a noun expressing an
  abstract quality (see *What is an Adjective?*, p. 99).

ADJECTIVE		FEMININE NOUN	
schön	*beautiful*	die Schön**heit**	*beauty*
frei	*free*	die Frei**heit**	*freedom*
möglich	*possible*	die Möglich**keit**	*possibility*

VERBS FORMED WITH PREFIXES

The infinitive form of a verb is always one word, i.e., the prefix
is part of the verb: **aus**gehen *(to go out)*, **be**suchen *(to visit)*.
However, that is not always the case when the verb is conjugated (see *What is a Verb Conjugation?*, p. 45). Prefixes are
divided into two groups depending on whether or not they
can be separated from the verb.

- **Separable prefixes** — German verbs with separable prefixes   80
  are similar to English verbs that are regularly used with a
  preposition (see *What is a Preposition?*, p. 64); namely, they
  are separate words functioning as a unit with the verb.

  They *are going out* tonight at 7:00 P.M.
  |
  preposition

  He *picks up* his friend after class.
  |
  preposition

  Separable prefixes in German include the following: **ab-,
  an-, auf-, aus-, bei-, ein-, fort-, her-, hin-, mit-, nach-,**   90
  um-, vor, weg-, weiter-, zurück-, zusammen-. Let us look
  at two examples to see how these prefixes can be separated
  from the verb.

INFINITIVE	SENTENCE
ausgehen	Hans und ich **gehen** morgen **aus**.
(to go out)	*Hans and I **are going out** tomorrow.*
ankommen	Der Zug **kommt** heute spät **an**.
(to arrive)	*The train **is arriving** late today.*

- **Inseparable prefixes** — German verbs with inseparable pre-   100
  fixes function as one word since these prefixes are never
  separated from the basic verb. Inseparable prefixes in
  German include the following: **be-, emp-, ent-, er-, ge-,**
  miss-, ver-, zer-. Let us look at two examples.

INFINITIVE	SENTENCE
besuchen	Wir **besuchen** unsere Tante.
(to visit)	*We **are visiting** our aunt.*
vergessen	Du **vergißt** immer dein Buch.
(to forget)	*You always **forget** your book.*

Your German textbook will explain the rules for using verbs   110
with separable and inseparable prefixes. When you learn a new
verb formed with a prefix, memorize whether the prefix is separable or not.

STUDY TIPS — PREFIXES AND SUFFIXES

Flashcards

1. Create flashcards of German verbal prefixes (**an-, mit-, ver-, ent-,** etc.).
   On the back of the card, write "Sep" (separable) or "Insep" (inseparable).
   If the prefix is easily translated, add the English translation. Underneath,
   write an example word using that prefix.   120

   mit-   Sep; *with*
           mitkommen *(to come along)*

ver-   Insep
verstehen *(to understand)*

2. Create another set of flashcards. On the German side, write the infinitive of the verb stem at the top of the card. Underneath it, make two columns: one for the verb stem with separable prefixes, the other for the verb stem with inseparable prefixes. On the back, using the same layout, write the English translations.

VERB STEM: stehen   *to stand*

SEP. PREFIX	INSEP. PREFIX		
aufstehen	bestehen	*to stand up*	*to pass a test*
anstehen	verstehen	*to stand in line*	*to understand*

Practice

1. Learn the meaning of the verb stem by flipping the cards first on the German side and then on the English side (see *Tips for Learning Vocabulary*, pp. 2-4).

2. Learn the meaning of the verbs with prefixes by flipping cards as under #1. Occasionally, the meaning of the prefixes will give you a clue as to the change of meaning of the verb stem.

3. Do the above exercises orally as the verb forms with separable prefixes are pronounced differently from those with inseparable prefixes: if the prefix is separable, it is the stressed part of the verb form (**auf**stehen); if the prefix is inseparable, it is the verb stem that is the stressed part of the verb form (ver**stehen**).

WHAT IS MEANT BY NUMBER?

NUMBER in the grammatical sense means that a word can be classi-   1
fied as singular or plural. When a word refers to one person or
thing, it is said to be SINGULAR; when it refers to more than one, it is
PLURAL.

> one *book*   two *books*
> | |
> singular   plural

More parts of speech indicate number in German than in English,
and there are also more spelling and pronunciation changes in
German than in English.

		10
ENGLISH	GERMAN
nouns	nouns
verbs	verbs
pronouns	pronouns
demonstrative adjectives	all adjectives
	articles

Since each part of speech follows its own rules to indicate number,
you will find number discussed in the sections dealing with articles, the various types of adjectives and pronouns, as well as in all
sections on verbs. In this section we will only look at number as it
is reflected in nouns.   20

IN ENGLISH

A singular noun is made plural in one of two ways.

- a singular noun can add an "-s" or "-es"

> book   book*s*
> kiss   kiss*es*

- a singular noun can change its spelling

> man   m*en*
> leaf   lea*ves*
> child   child*ren*   30

Some nouns, called COLLECTIVE NOUNS, refer to a group of persons
or things, but the noun itself is considered singular.

> A soccer *team* has eleven players.
> My *family* is well.

IN GERMAN

As in English, the plural form of German nouns is often spelled differently, and therefore pronounced differently, from the singular form. German plurals, however, are less predictable than English plurals; there are more endings and more internal spelling changes than in English. As you learn new nouns in German, you should memorize each noun's gender (see *What is Meant by Gender?*, p. 18) and its singular and plural forms. In the examples below, notice that besides adding different endings German often uses an **umlaut** (¨) to form plural nouns.

- singular noun + **-n** or **-en**

Auge	Aug**en**	*eye*	*eyes*
Frau	Frau**en**	*woman*	*wom**en***

- singular noun + **-e** (**umlaut** is sometimes added)

das Bein	die Bein**e**	*leg*	*legs*
der Stuhl	die Stüh**le**	*chair*	*chairs*

- singular noun + **-er** (**umlaut** added when the stem vowel is **a, o, u,** or **au**)

das Buch	die Bücher	*book*	*books*
das Haus	die Häuser	*house*	*houses*

- singular noun + no ending (**umlaut** added when the stem vowel is **a, o, u,** or **au**)

der Lehrer	die Lehrer	*teacher*	*teachers*
der Vater	die Väter	*father*	*fathers*

STUDY TIPS — NOUNS AND THEIR NUMBER

Flashcards

Sort out the flashcards for nouns (see p. 19) and add the plural form of the noun, preceded by the definite article *(What is an Article?*, p. 22).

Patterns

Learning the plural forms of German nouns will be easier if you can determine some patterns.

1. Create a short list of nouns that have the same ending in the singular. Write down the plural form beside each noun.

GROUP 1		GROUP 2	
Prüf**ung**	Prüf**ungen**	Winte**r**	Winte**r**
Wohn**ung**	Wohn**ungen**	Zimme**r**	Zimme**r**
Zeit**ung**	Zeit**ungen**	Lehre**r**	Lehre**r**

What pattern do you see?

- nouns ending in –**ung** add –**en** in the plural.
- nouns ending in –**er** do not change in the plural.

2. Try to determine some patterns of number based on the gender of the noun. Create lists of feminine and masculine nouns. Write the plural form beside each noun.

FEMININE	PLURAL
Schule	Schulen
Tür	Türen
Freiheit	Freiheiten
Spezialität	Spezialitäten
Freundschaft	Freundschaften

MASCULINE	PLURAL
Lehrer	Lehrer
Freund	Freunde
Bruder	Brüder

What pattern do you see?

- feminine nouns often use –n or –en to form the plural.
- feminine nouns formed with suffixes, -**keit**, –**heit**, -**tät**, and –**schaft** use
 –**en** to form the plural.
- some masculine nouns do not have any ending in the plural.
- masculine nouns often use an umlaut and/or an –**e** to form the plural.

3. Paying attention to the ending of a German noun will provide you with clues to both its gender and how to form its plural. The plural form of one noun can help you remember the plural form of another noun with the same ending.

CHAPTER

5

WHAT IS MEANT BY GENDER?

GENDER in the grammatical sense means that a word can be classified as masculine, feminine, or neuter.

> Did Franz give Ingrid the book? Yes, *he* gave *it* to *her*.
> masc. neuter fem.

Grammatical gender is not very important in English. However, it is at the very heart of the German language, where the gender of a word is often reflected not only in the word itself, but also in the way all the words connected to it are spelled and pronounced.

More parts of speech indicate gender in German than in English.

ENGLISH	GERMAN
pronouns	nouns
possessive adjectives	articles
	pronouns
	all adjectives

Since each part of speech follows its own rules to indicate gender, you will find gender discussed in the sections dealing with articles and with the various types of pronouns and adjectives. In this section we shall look at the gender of nouns only.

IN ENGLISH

Nouns themselves do not have gender, but sometimes their meaning indicates a gender based on the biological sex of the person or animal the noun represents. For example, when we replace a proper or common noun that refers to one man or woman, we use *he* for males and *she* for females.

- nouns and pronouns referring to males indicate the MASCULINE gender

> Lukas came home; *he* was happy; the dog was glad to see *him*.
> noun (male) masculine masculine

- nouns and pronouns referring to females indicate the FEMININE gender

> Anja came home; *she* was happy; the dog was glad to see *her*.
> noun (female) feminine feminine

All the proper or common nouns that are not perceived as having a biological gender are considered NEUTER and are replaced by *it* when they refer to one thing, place, or idea.

> The city of Munich is lovely. I enjoyed visiting *it*.
> noun neuter

IN GERMAN

All nouns—common nouns and proper nouns—have a gender; they are masculine, feminine, or neuter. Do not confuse the grammatical terms "masculine" and "feminine" with the terms "male" and "female." Only a few German nouns have a grammatical gender tied to whether they refer to someone of the male or female sex; most nouns have a gender that must be memorized.

The gender of most German nouns cannot easily be explained or figured out. These nouns have a grammatical gender that is unrelated to biological gender. Here are some examples of English nouns classified under the gender of their German equivalent.

MASCULINE	FEMININE	NEUTER
table	lamp	window
heaven	hope	girl
state	Switzerland	Germany
beginning	reality	topic

Textbooks and dictionaries usually indicate the gender of a noun with *m.* for masculine, *f.* for feminine, or *n.* for neuter. Sometimes definite articles are used: **der** for masculine, **die** for feminine, or **das** for neuter (see *What is an Article?*, p. 22).

A German noun will usually have different forms when it refers to the different sexes. For example, the noun *student* has two equivalents, a feminine form **Studentin** for females and a masculine form **Student** for males.

As you learn a new noun, you should always learn its gender because it will affect the form of the words related to it.

CAREFUL — Do not rely on biological gender to indicate the grammatical gender of German nouns that can refer to either a male or a female. For instance, the grammatical gender of the nouns **Kind** *(child)* and **Baby** *(baby)* is always neuter, even though the person being referred to could be male or female. Likewise, **Mädchen** *(girl)* always refers to a female but is neuter grammatically.

STUDY TIPS — NOUNS AND THEIR GENDER

Flashcards

1. Make a flashcard for each noun. You can do this by hand, or use a free online tool (simply search for "flash card maker"). Most online tools allow you to type in the information, practice with the cards online, and/or print out paper cards. For those with access to a Macintosh computer, consider making flashcards using Provoc (www.arizona-software.ch/provoc). This

40

50

60

70

80

free software allows you to move your flashcards onto an iPod for vocabulary practice on the go!

2. Use either colored paper or a highlighter to color code the flashcards
based on the gender of the noun: masculine = blue, feminine = red,
neuter = green. Associating the noun with blue, red, or green will help
you remember its gender.

3. On one side, write the German noun, including the singular article (see
What is an Article?, p. 22). On the other side, write the word in English or
use an image to depict the noun. You can find small images online at The
Internet Picture Dictionary (www.pdictionary.com/german), or photos of
objects in a German setting at the Culturally Authentic Pictorial Lexicon
(www.washjeff.edu/CAPL).

Pattern

Gender can sometimes be determined by looking at the ending of the
German noun. Here are some common endings you will want to notice.

MASCULINE ENDINGS

- all nouns referring to male persons that end in **-er, -ist, -ling, -ent**

der Physiker	*the physicist*
der Pianist	*the pianist*
der Jüngling	*the young man*
der Student	*the student*

- names of seasons (except **das Frühjahr**, *spring*), months, days, parts of
days (except **die Nacht**, *night*), geographical directions, and weather phe-
nomena

der Sommer	*summer*
der Januar	*January*
der Montag	*Monday*
der Mittag	*noon*
der Wind	*the wind*
der West	*west*

- most nouns which end in **-ig, -or, -ismus, -pf, -f, -ast, -ich**

der Pfennig	*the penny*
der Doktor	*the doctor*
der Optimismus	*optimism*
der Kopf	*the head*
der Senf	*mustard*
der Palast	*the palace*
der Teppich	*the carpet, the rug*

FEMININE ENDINGS

- most two-syllable nouns which end in **-e** (some common exceptions are
der Name, *the name*, **der Käse**, *the cheese*, **das Auge**, *the eye*)

die Lampe	*the lamp*
die Seife	*the soap*

- all nouns referring to female persons which end in **-in**

die Studentin	*the female student*
die Professorin	*the female Professor*

- all nouns ending in **-ei, -ie, -heit, -keit, -schaft, -ung, -ion, -tät, -ur, -ik, -a**

die Bücherei	*library*
die Drogerie	*drugstore*
die Dummheit	*stupidity*
die Möglichkeit	*possibility*
die Freundschaft	*friendship*
die Prüfung	*test*
die Reaktion	*reaction*
die Universität	*university*
die Natur	*nature*
die Musik	*music*
die Pizza	*pizza*

130

NEUTER ENDINGS

- all nouns ending in **-lein** or **-chen**

das Fräulein	*the young woman*
das Mädchen	*the young girl*

- all nouns ending in **-um, -ium** or **-tum**

das Studium	*study*
das Aluminium	*aluminum*
das Visum	*the visa*
das Eigentum	*property*
das Christentum	*Christianity*

140

- all nouns beginning with **Ge-**

das Gebäude	*the building*
das Gebet	*the prayer*
das Gelächter	*laughter*

- verb infinitives used as nouns (gerunds, see pp. 93-4)

das Lesen	*reading*
das Singen	

CHAPTER

6

WHAT IS AN ARTICLE?

An **ARTICLE** is a word placed before a noun to show whether the noun refers to a specific person, animal, place, thing, event, or idea, or whether the noun refers to an unspecified person, thing, or idea.

> I saw *the* video you spoke about.
> a specific video

> I saw *a* video at school.
> an unspecified video

In English and in German, there are two types of articles, definite articles and indefinite articles.

DEFINITE ARTICLES
IN ENGLISH
A **DEFINITE ARTICLE** is used before a noun when we are speaking about a particular person, place, animal, thing, event, or idea. There is one definite article, *the*.

> I read *the* book you recommended.
> a specific book

> Did you pass *the* exam?
> a specific exam

The definite article remains *the* when the noun that follows becomes plural.

> I read *the books* you recommended.

IN GERMAN
As in English, a definite article is used before a noun when referring to a specific person, place, animal, thing, or idea.

> Hast du **die Klausur** bestanden?
> *Did you pass **the exam**?*

In German, the article works hand-in-hand with the noun to which it belongs in that it matches the noun's gender, number, and case. This "matching" is called **AGREEMENT** (one says that "the article *agrees* with the noun"). See *What is Meant by Gender?*, p. 18, *What is Meant by Number?*, p. 15, and *What is Meant by Case?*, p. 28.

A different definite article is used, depending on three factors.

    1. GENDER — whether the noun is masculine, feminine, or neuter.

2. NUMBER — whether the noun is singular or plural.

3. CASE — the function of the noun in the sentence.

This chapter discusses only the basic form of the article as it is listed in the dictionary or in your textbook's vocabulary lists.

There are four forms of the definite article: three singular forms and one plural.

- **der** indicates that the noun is masculine singular
  der Baum   *the tree*

- **die** indicates that the noun is feminine singular
  die Tür   *the door*

- **das** indicates that the noun is neuter singular
  das Haus   *the house*

- **die** is also the definite article for all plural nouns
  die Türen   *the doors*

Since the same definite article **die** is used with feminine singular nouns and with plural nouns, you will have to rely on other indicators to determine the number of the noun. The most common indicator is the form of the noun itself: is it the singular form or the plural form?

> die **Tür**
> *the **door***
>> **Tür** is a singular noun; therefore, **die** is feminine singular.

> die **Türen**
> *the **doors***
>> **Türen** is a plural noun; therefore, **die** is plural.

You will discover other indicators of number as you learn more German (see *What is a Verb Conjugation?*, p. 45).

INDEFINITE ARTICLES
IN ENGLISH

An indefinite article is used before a noun when we are speaking about an unspecified person, animal, place, thing, event, or idea. There are two indefinite articles, *a* and *an*.

- *a* is used before a word beginning with a consonant
  I saw *a* video at school.
  not a specific video

- *an* is used before a word beginning with a vowel or a vowel sound
  I passed *an* exam.
  not a specific exam

She is taking *an* honors class.

not a specific honors class

The indefinite article is used only with a singular noun; it is dropped when the noun becomes plural. At times the word *some* is used to replace it, but it is usually omitted.

I saw videos at school.
I saw *(some)* videos at school.

I passed exams in all of my classes.

IN GERMAN

As in English, an indefinite article is used before a noun when we are not speaking about a specific person, animal, place, thing, event, or idea. As in English, the indefinite article is used only with a singular noun. Just as with German definite articles, indefinite articles must agree with the noun in gender, number, and case. There are two forms of the indefinite article.

- **ein** indicates that the noun is masculine or neuter

  ein Baum   *a tree*

  masculine

  ein Haus   *a house*

  neuter

- **eine** indicates that the noun is feminine

  eine Tür   *a door*

  feminine

Your textbook will instruct you on the different forms of the definite and indefinite articles in greater detail.

STUDY TIPS — NOUNS AND ARTICLES

Flashcards

1. Use your noun flashcards to memorize the meaning of the noun and the correct form of the definite article. As you look at the English side, say the definite article + noun out loud in German.
2. Repeat the above, this time using the plural definite article + the plural form of the noun.
3. Repeat the above, this time using the indefinite article + the singular form of the noun. Add an adjective such as **klein** *(small)* whose ending changes according to whether it precedes a masculine (**der, -er**), feminine (**die, -e**), or neuter (**das, -es**) noun. The change in ending of the adjective will reinforce the noun's gender in your memory.

     ein kleiner Hund (m.)   *a small dog*
     eine kleine Katze (f.)   *a small cat*
     ein kleines Kind (n.)   *a small child*

WHAT IS A VERB?

A **VERB** is a word that indicates the action of the sentence. The word   1
"action" is used in its broadest sense; it is not necessarily a physical
action. Let us look at different types of words that are verbs.

- a physical activity   to run, to hit, to talk, to walk
- a mental activity   to hope, to believe, to imagine, to dream, to think
- a condition   to be, to have, to seem

Many verbs, however, do not fall neatly into one of the above
three categories. They are verbs nevertheless because they represent the "action" of the sentence.   10

The book *costs* only $10.00.
                    |
        to cost

The table *seats* eight.
              |
        to seat

The verb is the most important word in a sentence. You cannot
write a **COMPLETE SENTENCE**, that is, express a complete thought,
without a verb.

It is important to identify verbs because the function of a word in
a sentence often depends on its relationship to the verb. For   20
instance, the subject of a sentence is the word doing the action of
the verb and the object is the word receiving the action of the verb
(see *What is a Subject?*, p. 40, and *What is an Object?*, p. 55).

IN ENGLISH

The basic form of a verb is called the **INFINITIVE**: *(to) eat, (to) sleep,
(to) drink*. In the dictionary the infinitive is listed without the
"to": *eat, sleep, drink*. When the infinitive is used in a sentence it
is always accompanied by another verb that is conjugated (see
What is a Verb Conjugation?, p. 45).

                                                      30

To study is challenging.
   |_____| |
  infinitive conjugated verb

It *is* important *to be* on time.
   | |___|
  conjugated verb infinitive

Axel and Jade *want to play* tennis.
                | |____|
          conjugated verb infinitive

After verbs such as *must, let, should,* and *can,* English uses the dictionary form of the verb without *to.*

> Gabi *must do* her homework.
> dictionary form

> The parents *let* the children *open* the presents.
> dictionary form

To help you learn to recognize verbs, look at the paragraph below where the verbs are in italics.

> The three students *entered* the restaurant, *selected* a table, *hung* up their coats, and *sat* down. They *looked* at the menu and *asked* the waitress what she *recommended*. She *named* the daily special, beef stew. It *was* not expensive. The service *was* slow, but the food *tasted* very good. Good cooking, they *decided, takes* time. They *ate* pastry for dessert and *finished* the meal with coffee.

IN GERMAN

As in English, verbs play an essential role in a sentence. The infinitive is the form under which verbs are listed in the dictionary; e.g., **arbeiten,** *to work.* (Notice that the English equivalent of a German infinitive is always preceded by *to.*) Sometimes German infinitives are preceded by **zu (zu arbeiten).** Your textbook will explain when **zu** is necessary. As in English, the infinitive is always used with the conjugated form of another verb.

The infinitive form always ends with the letters **-n** or **-en.**

> *Axel wants **to play** tennis.*
> Axel will Tennis **spielen.**
> conjugated verb   infinitive

> *Lukas does not want **to do** that.*
> Lukas will das nicht **tun.**
> conjugated verb   infinitive

You will find several examples of how verbs function differently in German and in English in the sections *What is an Object?*, p. 55, and *What are Reflexive Pronouns and Verbs?*, p. 80.

TERMS TO TALK ABOUT VERBS

- **Infinitive** or **dictionary form** — The verb form that is the name of the verb is called an infinitive: *(to) eat, (to) sleep, (to) drink.*
- **Conjugation** — A verb is conjugated or changes in form to agree with its subject: *I do, he does* (see *What is a Verb Conjugation?*, p. 45).

- **Tense** — A verb indicates tense, that is, the time (present, past, or future) of the action: *I am, I was, I will be* (see *What is Meant by Tense?*, p. 52).
- **Mood** — A verb shows mood, that is, the speaker's perception that what he or she is saying is fact, command, possibility, or wish (see *What is Meant by Mood?*, p. 150).
- **Voice** — A verb shows voice, that is, the relation between the subject and the action of the verb (see *What is Meant by Active and Passive Voice?*, p. 159).
- **Participle** — A verb may be used to form a participle: *writing, written, singing, sung* (see *What is a Participle?*, p. 90).
- **Transitive** or **intransitive** — A verb can be classified as transitive or intransitive depending on whether or not the verb can take a direct object (see pp. 55-6 in *What is an Object?*).

CHAPTER

8

WHAT IS MEANT BY CASE?

1   CASE in the grammatical sense means that a different form of the
word is used depending on the word's function in the sentence.

> *I* see Axel in class.
>
> the person speaking
> function → subject

> Axel sees *me* in class.
>
> the person speaking
> function → object

In the sentences above, the person speaking is referred to by the
10   forms "I" and "me." Different forms are used because in each sentence the person speaking has a different grammatical function. In
the first sentence, *I* is used because the person speaking is doing
the "seeing" and in the second sentence *me* is used because the
person speaking is the object of the "seeing."

More parts of speech are affected by case in German than in English.

ENGLISH	GERMAN
pronouns	nouns
	all pronouns
	adjectives
20 | | articles |

FUNCTION OF WORDS

The grammatical role of a word in a sentence is called its FUNCTION.
The function is often based on the word's relationship to the verb
(see *What is a Verb?*, p. 25). Here is a list of the various functions a
word can have, with reference to the section in this handbook
where each function is studied in detail.

- **Subject** — A noun or pronoun that performs the action of a verb
  (see *What is a Subject?*, p. 40, and *What is a Subject Pronoun?*, p. 41).
- **Predicate noun** — A noun that is linked to the subject by a
30   linking verb (see *What is a Predicate Noun?*, p. 43).
- **Object** — A noun or pronoun that is the receiver of the action of
  a verb (see *What is an Object?*, p. 55). There are different types of
  objects: direct objects (see p. 55), indirect objects (p. 57), and
  objects of a preposition (see p. 64).

To understand the meaning of a sentence, we must identify the
function of the various words that make up the sentence. In English, the function of a word is usually indicated by where it is

placed in a sentence. In German, where word order changes more often, the function of a word is marked by its case form.

Knowing how to analyze the function of words in an English sentence will help you to establish which case is required in the German sentence.

IN ENGLISH

English nouns do not change form to indicate different functions (see *What is a Noun?*, p. 9). For instance, the same form of the noun is used if it is the doer of the action (the subject) or the receiver of the action (the object). The function of a noun in a sentence is indicated by where it is placed in the sentence.

We easily recognize the difference in meaning between the following two sentences purely on the basis of word order.

> *The student* gives *the professor* the essay.
>> Here the student is giving the essay and the professor is receiving it.

> *The professor* gives *the student* the essay.
>> Here the professor is giving the essay and the student is receiving it.

These two sentences show how we can change the function of a noun by changing its place in the sentence, and consequently change the meaning of the sentence. As we shall see below, that is not the case with English pronouns.

In English the function of a personal pronoun is indicated not only by its place in the sentence, but also by its case (see *What is a Personal Pronoun?*, p. 36). As you can see in the two examples below, both the word order and the form of the pronoun give the sentence meaning.

> *I* know *them.*
> *They* know *me.*

We cannot say, "*I* know *they*" or "*They* know *I*" because the forms "they" and "I" can only be used to refer to the person doing the action. If you learn to recognize the different cases of pronouns in English, it will help you understand the German case system.

English pronouns have three cases.

- **Nominative case** — This case is used when a pronoun is a subject or replaces a predicate nominative (see *What is a Subject?*, p. 40, and *What is a Predicate Noun?*, p. 43).

> *She* and *I* went to the movies.
> └─────┘
>   subjects
>   nominative

40
50
60
70
80

It was *he* who did the deed.

predicate
nominative case

- **Objective case** — This case is used when a pronoun is an object (see *What is an Object?*, p. 55).

Axel saw *him*.

object
objective case

Alex sent *them* a note.

object
objective case

- **Possessive case** — This case is used when a pronoun shows ownership (see *What is a Possessive Pronoun?*, p. 114).

Is this book *yours*?

possessive case

Julia called her parents, but I wrote *mine* an e-mail.

possessive case

IN GERMAN

Unlike in English where only pronouns change form to indicate case, in German many parts of speech change form depending on the function of the word in the sentence. The case of a German word is sometimes reflected not only by the form of the word itself, but also by the form of the words that accompany it. We have limited the examples in this section to the case of nouns and their accompanying articles (see *What is a Noun?*, p. 9, and *What is an Article?*, p. 22).

German has four different cases, and each case reflects a different function of the word in a sentence.

- **Nominative case** — This case is used for the subject of a sentence and for predicate nouns (see *What is a Subject?*, p. 40, and *What is a Predicate Noun?*, p. 43). It is the form of nouns listed in a vocabulary list or a dictionary. This case corresponds to the nominative case in English.

- **Accusative case** — This case is used for most direct objects and after certain prepositions (see *What is an Object?*, p. 55, and *What is a Preposition?*, p. 64). The accusative and the dative below correspond to the objective case in English.

- **Dative case** — This case is used primarily for indirect objects, after certain prepositions, and after certain verbs (see p.56 in *What is an Object?*). The dative and the accusative above correspond to the objective case in English.

- **Genitive case** — This case is used to show possession or close relation, and after certain prepositions (see *What is the Possessive?*, p. 108). The genitive corresponds to the possessive forms in English.

The case of a noun is most often indicated by the ending of the accompanying article (see *What is an Article?*, p. 22); however, the form of the noun itself can also change. Each case has a singular and plural form (see *What is Meant by Number?*, p. 15). The complete set of case forms for any noun and its article is called the noun's DECLENSION. When you have memorized these forms, you are able to "decline" that noun.

Case affects the form of masculine and neuter nouns in the genitive singular and of all nouns in the dative plural.

- masculine and neuter singular nouns, genitive singular → add –(e)s

NOMINATIVE	GENITIVE
Mann (m. sing.)	Mannes
Kind (neut. sing.)	Kindes
Studium (neut. sing.)	Studiums

- all nouns, dative plural → add –n (if they don't already end with –n)

NOMINATIVE	DATIVE
Männer (m. pl.)	Männern
Kinder (neut. pl.)	Kindern
Frauen (f. pl.)	Frauen

Refer to your textbook for a small group of nouns called WEAK NOUNS or N-NOUNS that add -en to every case, except in the nominative. While small in number, some of these words, like **Student**, are common.

When case is not indicated by the form of the noun itself, it is the definite or indefinite article that accompanies the noun that reflects the case, number, and gender of the noun.

- masculine singular articles → four case forms

	DEF.	INDEF.
NOM.	der	ein
ACC.	den	einen
DAT.	dem	einem
GEN.	des	eines

- feminine singular articles → two case forms

	DEF.	INDEF.
NOM. & ACC.	die	eine
DAT. & GEN.	der	einer

130

140

150

160

- neuter singular articles → three case forms

	DEF.	INDEF.
NOM. & ACC.	das	ein
DAT.	dem	einem
GEN.	des	eines

- plural of all articles → three case forms

	DEF.	INDEF.
NOM. & ACC.	die	keine
DAT.	den	keinen
GEN.	der	keiner

Below is a chart illustrating how nouns and their accompanying article work hand-in-hand to indicate case: in the singular, a masculine noun **der Mann** (*man*), a feminine noun **die Frau** (*woman*), and a neuter noun **das Kind** (*child*), and in the plural **die Kinder** *(children)* that serves all genders. Be sure to memorize this chart.

	SINGULAR			PLURAL
	MASCULINE	FEMININE	NEUTER	
NOMINATIVE	**der** Mann	**die** Frau	**das** Kind	**die** Kinder
ACCUSATIVE	**den** Mann	**die** Frau	**das** Kind	**die** Kinder
DATIVE	**dem** Mann	**der** Frau	**dem** Kind	**den** Kindern
GENITIVE	**des** Mannes	**der** Frau	**des** Kindes	**der** Kinder

To choose the appropriate case for nouns in a sentence, you need to go through a series of steps.

Here is an example.

> **The** *mother gives* **the** *child* **the** *apple.*

1. GENDER — Identify the gender and number of each noun.
   > *the mother* → **die Mutter**→ feminine singular
   > *the child* → **das Kind** → neuter singular
   > *the apple* → **der Apfel** → masculine singular

2. FUNCTION — Determine the function of each noun.
   > *the mother* → subject
   > *the child* → indirect object
   > *the apple* → direct object

3. CASE — Determine what case in German corresponds to the function identified in step 2.
   > *the mother* → subject → nominative case
   > *the apple* → direct object → accusative case
   > *the child* → indirect object → dative case

4. SELECTION — Choose the proper form from the declension you have memorized.

Die Mutter gibt **dem** Kind **den** Apfel. 210

feminine	neuter	masculine
singular	singular	singular
nominative	dative	accusative

Once the nouns are in their proper case, words in a sentence can be moved around without changing its meaning. Look at the many ways the English sentence above can be expressed in German.

Die Mutter gibt **dem** Kind **den** Apfel.
the mother gives to the child the apple

Den Apfel gibt **die** Mutter **dem** Kind. 220
Dem Kind gibt **die** Mutter **den** Apfel.

SUMMARY

- *who* or *what* is doing the action of the verb → subject → nominative case
- *who* or *what* is the direct recipient of the action of the verb → direct object → accusative case (a few verbs take the dative case see p. 56, l. 65)
- *who* or *what* is the indirect recipient of the action of the verb → indirect object → dative case
- *something* belongs to *someone* → possession → genitive case 230

Your textbook will explain in greater detail how to use the different case forms for the definite and indefinite articles. As you learn more German, you will discover other ways in which case affects the form of nouns, pronouns, and adjectives (see *What is an Adjective?*, p. 99).

STUDY TIPS — CASE

Flashcards

Using the chart on p. 32, make cards illustrating each case by writing the German noun and accompanying article on one side; on the other side, indicate the gender, case, and number of the noun. 240

dem Kind	neuter, dative, singular
einer Frau	feminine, dative or genitive, singular
die Kinder	neuter, nominative or accusative, plural

While most case endings are duplicated on the chart, notice that -m only occurs in the dative singular and that **-es** only occurs in the genitive singular for the masculine and neuter genders.

CHAPTER

9

WHAT IS A PRONOUN?

A **PRONOUN** is a word used in place of one or more nouns. It may stand, therefore, for a person, place, thing, or idea.

> *Karen* likes to sing. *She* practices every day.
> noun   pronoun

In the example above, the pronoun *she* refers to the proper noun *Karen* (see *What is a Noun?*, p. 9). A pronoun is almost always used to refer to someone, something, or an idea that has already been mentioned. The word that the pronoun replaces is called the **ANTECEDENT** of the pronoun. *Karen* is the antecedent of the pronoun *she*.

IN ENGLISH

There are different types of pronouns, each serving a different function and following different rules. The list below presents the most important types and refers you to the section where they are discussed.

PERSONAL PRONOUNS — These pronouns refer to different persons or things (i.e., *me, you, her, it*) and they change their form according to the function they have in a sentence (see pp. 29-30). The personal pronouns include:

Subject pronouns — These pronouns are used as the subject of a verb (see p. 41).

> *I* go.
> *They* read.
> *He* runs.

Object pronouns — These pronouns are used as:

- direct objects of a verb (see p. 55)

> Tina loves *him*.
> Mark saw *them* at the theater.

- indirect objects of a verb (see p. 57)

> The boy wrote *me* the letter.
> Petra gave *us* the book.

- objects of a preposition (see p. 64)

> Angela is going to the movies with *us*.
> Don't step on it; walk around *it*.

REFLEXIVE PRONOUNS — These pronouns refer back to the subject of the sentence (see p. 80).

> I cut *myself.*
> She spoke about *herself.*   40

INTERROGATIVE PRONOUNS — These pronouns are used in questions (see p. 118).

> *Who* is that?
> *What* do you want?

POSSESSIVE PRONOUNS — These pronouns are used to show possession (see p. 114).

> Whose book is that? *Mine.*
> *Yours* is on the table.

RELATIVE PRONOUNS — These pronouns are used to introduce relative subordinate clauses (see p. 142).   50

> The man *who* came is very nice.
> Ingrid, *whom* you met, wants to study in Berlin.

IN GERMAN

Pronouns are identified in the same way as in English. The most important difference is that German pronouns have more forms than English pronouns since they must agree in gender, number, and case with the nouns they replace (see *What is Meant by Gender?*, p. 18, *What is Meant by Number?*,   60 p. 15, *What is Meant by Case?*, p. 28, and *What is a Subject Pronoun?*, p. 41).

You'll find a detailed discussion of German pronouns in the chapters referred to under In English above.

WHAT IS A PERSONAL PRONOUN?

A **PERSONAL PRONOUN** is a word used to refer to a person or thing that has previously been mentioned.

> Axel reads a book. *He* reads *it*.
>> *He* is a pronoun replacing a person, *Axel*.
>> *It* is a pronoun replacing a thing, *book*.

Personal pronouns can function as subjects, objects, and objects of prepositions. These functions are discussed in separate sections: *What is a Subject Pronoun?*, p. 41, *What are Direct and Indirect Object Pronouns?*, p. 59, and *What is an Object of Preposition Pronoun?*, p. 69.

In English and in German, personal pronouns, as well as other parts of speech, are often referred to by the **PERSON** to which they belong: 1st, 2nd, or 3rd and singular or plural. The word "person" in this instance is a grammatical term that does not necessarily mean a human being; it can also mean a thing.

IN ENGLISH

Each of the six "persons" is used to refer to one or more persons or things. We have listed them in the order in which they are usually presented and given the equivalent subject pronoun. Sometimes, as in the case of the 3rd person singular, more than one pronoun *(he, she,* and *it)* belongs to the same person.

1ST PERSON

I → person speaking → SINGULAR
we → person speaking plus others → PLURAL
> *Hans and I* are free this evening. *We* are going out.

2ND PERSON

you → person or persons spoken to → SINGULAR or PLURAL
> *Lukas*, do *you* sing folk songs?
> *Johan, Kurt and Tina*, do *you* sing folk songs?

3RD PERSON

he, she, it → person or object spoken about → SINGULAR
they → persons or objects spoken about → PLURAL
> *Lukas* cannot come along. *He* has to work.
> *Tina and Axel* are free this evening. *They* are going out.

As you can see above, all the personal pronouns, except *you*, show whether one person or more than one is involved. For instance, the singular *I* is used by the person who is speaking to

refer to himself or herself, and the plural *we* is used by the
person speaking to refer to himself or herself plus others.

IN GERMAN

German personal pronouns are also identified as 1st, 2nd, and 3rd
persons, each having a singular and a plural form. They are
usually presented in the following order:

SINGULAR

1st PERSON	*I*	ich	
2nd PERSON	*you*	du	FAMILIAR
		Sie	FORMAL
3RD PERSON	*he*	er	MASCULINE
	she	sie	FEMININE
		er	MASCULINE
	it	sie	FEMININE
		es	NEUTER

PLURAL

1ST PERSON	*we*	wir	
2ND PERSON	*you*	ihr	FAMILIAR
		Sie	FORMAL
3RD PERSON	*they*	sie	

CHOOSING THE CORRECT "PERSON"

Let us look at the English pronouns that have more than one
equivalent in German: *you* and *it*.

"You"

IN ENGLISH

The same pronoun "you" is used to address one or more than
one person.

> Ann, are *you* coming with me?
> Ann and Lukas, are *you* coming with me?

The same pronoun "you" is used to address anyone (person or
animal), regardless of their rank.

> Do *you* have any questions, Mr. President?
> *You* are a good dog, Spot.

IN GERMAN

There are two sets of pronouns for *you,* the FAMILIAR FORM and
the FORMAL FORM.

Familiar "you" → du or ihr

The familiar forms of *you* are used to address members of one's
family (notice that the word "familiar" is similar to the word
"family"), persons you call by their first name, children, and pets.

- to address one person (2nd person singular) → **du**

    Jade, are *you* there?
    |
    du

    Axel, are *you* there?
    |
    du

- to address more than one person (2nd person plural) to whom you would say **du** individually → **ihr**

    Jade and Axel, are *you* there?
    |
    ihr

Formal "you" → Sie

The formal form of *you* is used to address persons you do not know well enough to call by their first name or to whom you should show respect (Ms. Smith, Mr. Jones, Dr. Anderson, Professor Schneider). There is only one form, **Sie**, regardless of whether you are addressing one or more persons.

    Professor Schneider, are *you* there?
    |
    Sie

    Professor Schneider and Mrs. Schneider, are *you* there?
    |
    Sie

Note that the formal *you* form **Sie** is always capitalized. It should help you distinguish it from **sie** the German pronoun for *she* and for *they*.

If in doubt as to whether to use the familiar or formal form when addressing an adult, use the formal form. It shows respect for the person you are talking to, and the use of the familiar form might be considered rude.

"It"

IN ENGLISH

Whenever you are speaking about one thing or idea, you use the personal pronoun *it*.

    Where is the pencil? *It* is on the table.
    Axel has an idea. *It* is very interesting.

When there is no reference to a specific noun, you use *it*.

    It is raining.

IN GERMAN

The personal pronoun used depends on the gender of the German noun *it* replaces, i.e., its antecedent. Thus *it* can be either masculine, feminine, or neuter (see *What is Meant by Gender?*, p. 18).

To choose the correct form of *it*, you must identify two things:

1. ANTECEDENT — Find the noun *it* replaces.
2. GENDER — Determine the gender of the German word for the antecedent.

Here are some examples.

- masculine antecedent → **er**

  Where is the suitcase? It is next to the chair.
  > ANTECEDENT: the suitcase
  > GENDER: **Der Koffer** *(suitcase)* is masculine.

  Wo ist der Koffer? **Er** ist neben dem Stuhl.

masculine

- feminine antecedent → **sie**

  How was the trip ? It was nice.
  > ANTECEDENT: the trip
  > GENDER: **Die Reise** *(trip)* is feminine.

  Wie war die Reise? **Sie** war sehr schön.

feminine

- neuter antecedent → **es**

  When does the plane leave? It leaves at 10 o'clock.
  > ANTECEDENT: the plane
  > GENDER: **Das Flugzeug** *(plane)* is neuter.

  Wann fliegt das Flugzeug ab? **Es** fliegt um 10 Uhr ab.

neuter

- no reference to a specific noun → **es**

  It is raining.
  Es regnet.

neuter

In both English and German personal pronouns have different forms to show their function in a sentence; these forms are called CASE FORMS (see *What is Meant by Case?*, p. 28).

STUDY TIPS — PERSONAL PRONOUNS

Flashcards
Make a flashcard for each personal pronoun, with a separate card for the four forms of *you*: singular familiar; singular formal; plural familiar; plural formal.

CHAPTER

11

WHAT IS A SUBJECT?

In a sentence the person or thing that performs the action of the verb is called the SUBJECT.

IN ENGLISH

To find the subject of a sentence, always look for the verb first; then ask, *who?* or *what?* before the verb (see *What is a Verb?*, p. 25). The answer will be the subject.

> Axel studies German.
>> VERB: studies
>> *Who* studies German? ANSWER: Axel.
>> *Alex* is the subject.
>> The subject is singular (see p. 15). It refers to one person.

> Did the packages come yesterday?
>> VERB: come
>> *What* came yesterday? ANSWER: packages.
>> *Packages* is the subject.
>> The subject is plural. It refers to more than one thing.

If a sentence has more than one main verb, you have to find the subject of each verb.

> The boys were cooking while Jade set the table.
>> *Boys* is the subject of *were*.
>> Note that the subject is plural.
>> *Jade* is the subject of *set*.
>> Note that the subject is singular.

IN GERMAN

In German it is particularly important that you recognize the subject of a sentence so that you can put it in the proper case (see *What is Meant by Case?*, p. 28). The subject of a German sentence is in the nominative case.

> **Das Kind** spielt allein.
> *The child plays alone.*
>> Who plays? ANSWER: the child
>> Child (**das Kind**) is the subject, therefore **das Kind** is in the nominative case.

CAREFUL — In English and in German it is important to find the subject of each verb so that you can choose the form of the verb that goes with each subject (see *What is a Verb Conjugation?*, p. 45).

WHAT IS A SUBJECT PRONOUN?

Pronouns used as subjects are called SUBJECT PRONOUNS (see *What is a*   1
Subject?, p. 40).

> *They* ran, but *I* walked.
>> Who ran? ANSWER: They.
>> *They* is the subject of the verb *ran*.
>> Who walked? ANSWER: I.
>> *I* is the subject of the verb *walked*.

IN ENGLISH

Below is a list of English subject pronouns, also referred to as
NOMINATIVE PRONOUNS. For an explanation of the various "persons" see p. 36.   10

SINGULAR
1ST PERSON	I
2ND PERSON	you
3RD PERSON	he, she, it

PLURAL
1ST PERSON	we
2ND PERSON	you
3RD PERSON	they

The above personal pronouns are used as subjects of a verb or as
predicate nominatives (see p. 43). English uses another set of   20
pronouns when the pronoun is an object of a verb or a preposition (see *What are Direct and Indirect Object Pronouns?*, p. 59, and
What is an Object of Preposition Pronoun?, p. 69).

IN GERMAN

The NOMINATIVE CASE of the pronoun is used as subject of the
verb (see *What is a Verb?*, p. 25, and p. 30 in *What is Meant by
Case?*).   30

	ENGLISH	GERMAN NOMINATIVE	
SINGULAR			
1ST PERSON	*I*	ich	
2ND PERSON	*you*	du	FAMILIAR
		Sie	FORMAL
3RD PERSON	*he*	er	MASCULINE
	she	sie	FEMININE
	it	er	MASCULINE
		sie	FEMININE
		es	NEUTER

40

PLURAL

1ˢᵗ PERSON	*we*	wir	
2ᴺᴰ PERSON	*you*	⎧ ihr	FAMILIAR
		⎩ Sie	FORMAL
3ᴿᴰ PERSON	*they*	sie	

To help you select the proper German subject pronoun, see pp. 37-9 in *What is a Personal Pronoun?.*

WHAT IS A PREDICATE NOUN?

A **PREDICATE NOUN** is a noun connected to the subject by a linking   1
verb. A **LINKING VERB** is a verb that acts as an equal sign linking
interchangeable elements. (See *What is a Noun?*, p. 9, and *What is a
Verb?*, p. 25).

> Johan is my friend. [Johan = friend]
> subject | predicate noun
>   linking verb

IN ENGLISH

The most common linking verbs are *to be* and *to become.* The
noun that follows the linking verb is not an object because it   10
does not receive the action of the verb (see *What is an Object?*,
p. 55); instead, it is a predicate noun because it is interchangeable with the subject.

> Ingrid is a good *student.*
>   linking verb   predicate noun
>   LINKING VERB: is (form of *to be*)
>   SUBJECT: Ingrid
>   PREDICATE NOUN: student (Ingrid = student)

> Axel became a *teacher.*
>   linking verb   predicate noun   20
>   LINKING VERB: became (form of *to become*)
>   SUBJECT: Axel
>   PREDICATE NOUN: teacher (Axel = teacher)

IN GERMAN

The most common linking verbs are **sein** *(to be)*, **werden** *(to
become)* and **scheinen** *(to appear).* As in English, the noun following a linking verb is a predicate noun, not an object. Predicate nouns are in the nominative case, the same case as the subject (see *What is Meant by Case?*, p. 28).

> Ingrid ist eine gute **Studentin.**   30
> nom.   linking   nom.
> case   verb   case
>   LINKING VERB: **ist** (form of **sein** *to be*)
>   SUBJECT = PREDICATE NOUN: **Ingrid** = **Studentin** *(student)*
>   Both **Ingrid** and **Studentin** are in the nominative case.
> *Ingrid is a good **student.***

Axel wurde **Lehrer.**

nom.   linking   nom.
case   verb   case

> LINKING VERB: **wurde** (form of **werden** *to become*)
> SUBJECT = PREDICATE NOUN: **Axel** = **Lehrer** *(teacher)*
> Both **Axel** and **Lehrer** are in the nominative case.

*Axel became a **teacher.***

CAREFUL — It is important that you distinguish predicate nouns from objects so that you can put them in the appropriate case, i. e., the nominative case.

STUDY TIPS — PREDICATE NOUNS

Flashcards

On the English side of your cards for the verbs **sein, werden**, and **scheinen** indicate "linking verb, predicate noun takes nominative case (N), with an example.

Herr Meier ist der Lehrer.
N   N

WHAT IS A VERB CONJUGATION?

A **VERB CONJUGATION** is a list of the six possible forms of a verb for a par-   ₁
ticular tense (see *What is Meant by Tense?*, p. 52). For each tense, there
is one verb form for each of the six persons used as the subject of the
verb (see *What is a Subject Pronoun?*, p. 41).

> I am
> you are
> he, she, it is
> we are
> you are
> they are

Different tenses have different verb forms, but the principle of con-   10
jugation remains the same. In this chapter our examples are in the
present tense (see *What is the Present Tense?*, p. 54).

IN ENGLISH

The verb *to be* conjugated above is the English verb that changes
the most; it has three forms: *am, are,* and *is.* (In conversation the
initial vowel is often replaced by an apostrophe: *I'm, you're,
he's*). Other English verbs only have two forms. Let us look at
the verb *to sing.*

SINGULAR

1ˢᵀ PERSON	I sing	20
2ⁿᵈ PERSON	you sing	
3ᴿᴰ PERSON	he sings she sings it sings	

PLURAL

1ˢᵀ PERSON	we sing
2ⁿᵈ PERSON	you sing
3ᴿᴰ PERSON	they sing

Because English verbs change so little, it isn't necessary to learn
"to conjugate a verb;" that is, to list all its possible forms. For   30
most verbs, it is much simpler to say that the verb adds an "(e)-s"
in the 3ᴿᴰ person singular.

IN GERMAN

Unlike English, German verb forms change from one person to
another so that when you learn a new verb you must also learn
how to conjugate it. The conjugation of most verbs follow a predictable pattern, so that once you learn the pattern for one reg-

ular German verb you will be able to apply that pattern to other regular German verbs.

HOW TO CONJUGATE A VERB
A German verb is composed of two parts, a stem and an ending.

- **THE STEM** — the part of the verb left after dropping the final -**en** from the infinitive (or with a few verbs like **tun** and **ändern** by dropping the final -**n**).

INFINITIVE	STEM	IN CONJUGATION
singen	sing-	ich singe (1st pers. sing.)
machen	mach-	du machst (2nd pers. sing,)
kommen	komm-	sie kommt (3rd pers. sing.)

Listed below is the terminology used to categorize German verbs according to the changes in the stem. You will notice that some verbs belong to more than one category.

Regular verbs, also known as **weak verbs** — verbs that keep the same stem throughout the different tenses. For example, **wohnen, wohn**te, gewohnt *(live, lived, lived).*

Irregular verbs, also known as **strong verbs** — verbs whose stem vowel changes. There are different kinds of irregular verbs depending on when the stem vowel changes:

Stem-changing verbs — verbs whose stem vowel changes in the 2nd and 3rd person singular of the present tense. For example, **lesen** *(to read),* **du liest, er liest** *(you read, he reads).* The stem change can also be the addition of an umlaut over the vowel. For example, **fahren** *(to travel),* **du fährst, er fährt** *(you travel, he travels).*

Strong verbs — verbs whose stem vowel changes to indicate different tenses. For example, **singen, sang, gesung**en *(sing, sang, sung).*

Some verbs belong to the two above categories: for instance, **geben** *(to give)* is a stem-changing verb since the stem vowel changes from -**e**- to -**i**- in the 2nd and 3rd person singular in the present tense; it is also a strong verb since the stem vowel changes from -**e**- to **a**- depending on the tense.

Mixed verbs — verbs that have elements of both weak and strong verbs. Many common verbs are mixed verbs: **bringen** *(to bring),* **kennen** *(to know),* **denken** *(to think).*

When you learn a new verb, memorize in which category it belongs so that you can conjugate it correctly.

- **The ending** — the part of the verb that is added at the end of the stem and that corresponds to the grammatical person.

Here are the steps to conjugate the regular verb **machen** *(to make)* in the present tense.

1. Find the verb stem by removing the infinitive ending.

    INFINITIVE: **machen** → STEM: **mach-**

2. Add the ending that agrees with the subject. Regular and irregular verbs add the same endings in the present tense.

SINGULAR

1ST PERSON	ich mache	*I make*
2ND PERSON FAMILIAR	du machst	*you make*
	er macht	*he, it makes*
3RD PERSON	sie macht	*she, it makes*
	es macht	*it makes*

PLURAL

1ST PERSON	wir machen	*we make*
2ND PERSON FAMILIAR	ihr macht	*you make*
3RD PERSON	sie machen	*they make*
2ND PERSON FORMAL (sing. & pl.)	Sie machen	*you make*

As irregular verbs are introduced in your textbook, either their entire conjugation or their principal parts will be given so that you will know how to conjugate them (see *What are the Principal Parts of a Verb?*, p. 72). Be sure to memorize these forms, because many common verbs are irregular (**sein**, *to be;* **gehen**, *to go;* **werden**, *to become*, for example).

CHOOSING THE CORRECT "PERSON" (see p. 36)

In your textbook, the 2nd person formal forms will either be listed after the 2nd person familiar plural forms or after the 3rd person plural form, as they are in the conjugation of the verb **singen** *(to sing)* below.

SINGULAR

1ST PERSON	ich singe	*I sing*
2ND PERSON FAMILIAR	du singst	*you sing*
	er singt	*he, it sings*
3RD PERSON	sie singt	*she, it sings*
	es singt	*it sings*

PLURAL

1ST PERSON	wir singen	*we sing*
2ND PERSON FAMILIAR	ihr singt	*you sing*
3RD PERSON	sie singen	*they sing*
2ND PERSON FORMAL (sing. & pl.)	Sie singen	*you sing*

To choose the proper verb form, it is important to identify the person and the number of the subject.

1ˢᵀ person singular — The subject is always **ich** *(I)*.

> **Ich** singe leise.
> *I sing softly.*

Notice that **ich** is not capitalized, except when it is the first word of a sentence.

2ⁿᵈ person singular familiar — The subject is always **du** *(you)*.

> Katrin, **du** singst gut.
> *Katrin, **you** sing well.*

3ʳᵈ person singular — The subject can be expressed in one of three ways:

- the 3ʳᵈ person singular masculine pronoun **er** *(he or it)*, the feminine pronoun **sie** *(she or it)*, and the neuter pronoun **es** *(it)*

> **Er** singt schön.
> *He sings beautifully.*
>
> **Sie** singt schön.
> *She sings beautifully.*
>
> **Es** singt schön.
> *It sings beautifully.*

- a proper noun

> **Anna** singt gut.
> *Anna sings well.*
>
> **Der Fischer Chor** singt gut.
> *The Fischer choir sings well.*
>> The proper noun could be replaced by the pronoun *he, she* or *it* (**er, sie,** or **es**) → use the 3ʳᵈ person singular form of the verb.

- a singular common noun

> **Der Vogel** singt.
> *The bird sings.*
>
> **Die Geige** singt.
> *The violin sings.*
>
> **Das Kind** singt.
> *The child sings.*
>> The common noun could be replaced by the pronoun *he, she* or *it* (**er, sie,** or **es**) → use the 3ʳᵈ person singular form of the verb.

1ˢᵀ person plural — The subject can be expressed in one of two ways:

- the 1ˢᵀ person plural pronoun **wir** *(we)*

> **Wir** singen gut.
> *We sing well.*

130

140

150

160

- a multiple subject in which the speaker is included

   Axel, Lukas und ich singen gut.
   Axel, Lukas and I sing well.

   > The subjects, *Axel, Lukas* and *I*, could be replaced by the pronoun *we*   170
   > (**wir**) → use the 1ˢᵗ person plural form of the verb.

2ⁿᵈ person plural familiar — The subject is always **ihr** *(you).*

   Ingrid und Lukas, singt **ihr** auch?
   Ingrid and Lukas, do you sing too?

   > The subjects, *Ingrid* and *Lukas* (whom you would address with the 2ⁿᵈ
   > person familiar individually), could be replaced by the pronoun *you*
   > (**ihr**) → use the 2ⁿᵈ person plural familiar form of the verb.

2ⁿᵈ person formal (singular and plural) — The subject is always **Sie** *(you).*

   Frau Meier, wollen **Sie** heute nicht singen?   180
   Mrs. Meier, do you not want to sing today?

   Herr und Frau Meier, singen **Sie** gern zusammen?
   Mr. and Mrs. Meier, do you like to sing together?

   > The subjects, *Mr.* and *Mrs. Meier* (whom you would address with the
   > 2ⁿᵈ person formal individually or together), ∅could be replaced by
   > the pronoun *you* (**Sie**) → use the 2ⁿᵈ person formal form of the verb.

3ʳᵈ person plural — The subject can be expressed in one of three ways:

- the 3ʳᵈ person plural pronoun **sie** *(they)*

   Sie singen im Chor.   190
   They sing in the choir.

- a plural noun

   Die Kinder singen im Chor.
   The children sing in the choir.

   > The plural noun could be replaced by the 3ʳᵈ person plural pronoun
   > *they* (**sie**) → use the 3ʳᵈ person plural form of the verb..

- two or more proper or common nouns

   Lukas und Ingrid singen ein Duett.
   Lukas and Ingrid sing a duet.

   Die Gläser und Teller sind auf dem Tisch.   200
   The glasses and plates are on the table.

   > The nouns could be replaced by the 3ʳᵈ person plural pronoun *they*
   > (**sie**) → use the 3ʳᵈperson plural form of the verb.

STUDY TIPS — VERB CONJUGATIONS

Pattern (see *Tips for Learning Word Forms*, p. 4)

1. Start by looking for a pattern within the conjugation of the verb itself. For example, let's find a pattern in the regular verbs **wohnen** *(to live)* and **machen** *(to make)* above.

210

ich wohne	wir wohnen
du wohnst	ihr wohnt
er/sie/es wohnt	sie wohnen/Sie Wohnen

What pattern do you see?
- all the forms start with the same stem: **wohn-** and **mach-**
- **ich** forms have an -e ending
- **du** forms have an -st ending
- **er/sie/es** and **ihr** have a -t ending
- **wir, sie** (pl.) and **Sie** have an -en ending

If you learn best with mnemonics, think of the regular conjugation pattern as the verb stem + **-e, -st, 10, 10** throughout the list; that is, **-e, -st, -t, -en, -t, -en** for **ich, du, er/sie/es, wir, ihr,** and **Sie/sie**.

220

2. Whenever you learn a new verb, look for similarities with another verb.

The pattern can be related to the consonant ending the stem. For example, let's look at **fin_den** (to find), **arbei_ten** (to work) and **öff_nen** (to open).

ich finde	wir finden	ich arbeite	wir arbeiten	ich öffne	wir öffnen
du findest	ihr findet	du arbeitest	ihr arbeitet	du öffnest	ihr öffnet
er findet	sie/Sie finden	er arbeitet	sie/Sie arbeiten	er öffnet	sie/Sie öffnen

What similarities and differences with regular verbs (see under 1 above) do you see?
- the endings of the verb forms are the same, except for **du, er/sie/es** and **ihr** that insert an **-e** before the ending

230

The pattern can be related to the vowel of the stem. For example, let's look at three stem-changing verbs **s_e_hen** (to see), **schl_a_fen** (to sleep) and **g_e_ben** (to give).

ich sehe	wir sehen	ich schlafe	wir schlafen	ich gebe	wir geben
du siehst	ihr seht	du schläfst	ihr schlaft	du gibst	ihr gebt
er sieht	sie/Sie sehen	er schläft	sie/Sie schlafen	er gibt	sie/Sie geben

What similarities and differences with regular verbs (see under 1 above) do you see?
- the endings of all the verb forms are the same
- the stem vowel changes only in the **du** and **er/sie/es** forms
- vowels change in the same way in the **du** and **er/sie/es** forms

240

3. In the conjugation of most regular and irregular German verbs, there are four forms that look like the infinitive of the verb and end in **-en** or **-n**: the 1st and 3rd persons plural and the 2nd person formal, singular and plural (see p. 25 in *What is a Verb?*).

4. As new verb conjugations are introduced, more and more similarities and patterns will become evident. Take the time to look for them.

Flashcards

Create a card for each verb to memorize its meaning and conjugation pattern. On the German side, write the infinitive form and the following information as appropriate:

1. If it is a stem-changing verb, indicate its type (**a → ä; e → i; e → ie**) in parentheses.

250

fahren (a → ä)	*to drive*
geben (e → i)	*to give*
lesen (e → ie)	*to read*

2. If the verb requires a spelling change in the **du** or **er/sie/es** endings owing to particular consonant combinations, write the form in parentheses and underline the spelling change.

> reden (er red<u>et</u>)   *to talk*
> arbeiten (er arbeit<u>et</u>)   *to work*
> tanzen (du tan<u>z</u>t)   *to dance*

Practice

1. Learn the different forms of a verb by writing them down (always using the subject pronoun). Repeat until you can write the correct forms without referring to your textbook.

2. Practice using the various forms out of order, so that if you are asked a question you can respond without going through the entire pattern.

3. Be sure to do the exercises that follow the introduction of a new conjugation. When you've finished, refer to your textbook or answer key to make corrections. Mark the mistakes and corrections with a colored pen so that they stand out and you can concentrate on them when you review.

4. Write your own sentences using the different forms of the verb.

See also *Study Tips — Principal Parts of Verbs* (p. 74).

260

CHAPTER

15

WHAT IS MEANT BY TENSE?

The TENSE of a verb indicates when the action of the verb takes place: at the present time, in the past, or in the future.

I am studying	PRESENT
I studied	PAST
I will study	FUTURE

As you can see in the above examples, just by putting the verb in a different tense, and without giving any additional information (such as "I am studying *now*," "I studied *yesterday*," "I will study *tomorrow*"), you can indicate when the action of the verb takes place.

Tenses may be classified according to the way they are formed. A SIMPLE TENSE consists of only one verb form (I *studied),* while a COMPOUND TENSE consists of one or more auxiliaries plus the main verb (I *am studying, I have studied*). See *What is an Auxiliary Verb?*, p. 76.

In this section we will only consider tenses of the indicative mood (see *What is Meant by Mood?*, p. 150).

IN ENGLISH

Listed below are the main tenses of the indicative mood whose equivalents you will encounter in German.

PRESENT
I study	PRESENT
I am studying	PRESENT PROGRESSIVE
I do study	PRESENT EMPHATIC

PAST
I studied	SIMPLE PAST
I did study	PAST EMPHATIC
I have studied	PRESENT PERFECT
I was studying	PAST PROGRESSIVE
I had studied	PAST PERFECT

FUTURE
I will study	FUTURE
I will have studied	FUTURE PERFECT

As you can see, there are only two simple tenses: present and simple past. All the other tenses are compound tenses.

IN GERMAN

Listed below are the main tenses of the indicative mood that you will encounter in German.

PRESENT

ich studiere	*I study, I do study*	PRESENT
	I am studying	

PAST

ich studierte	{ *I studied,*	SIMPLE PAST/
	I was studying	IMPERFECT
ich habe studiert	*I have studied*	PRESENT PERFECT
ich hatte studiert	*I had studied*	PAST PERFECT

FUTURE

ich werde studieren	*I will study*	FUTURE
ich werde studiert haben	*I will have studied*	FUTURE PERFECT

As you can see, there are fewer present tense forms in German than in English; for example, there are no progressive forms.

This handbook discusses the various tenses and their usage in separate chapters: *What is the Present Tense?*, p. 54; *What is the Past Tense?*, p. 87; *What is the Future Tense?*, p. 85; *What is the Past Perfect Tense?*, p. 95; and *What is the Future Perfect Tense?*, p. 97. Verb tenses can be grouped according to the mood in which they are used.

CAREFUL — Do not assume that tenses with the same name are used the same way in English and in German.

CHAPTER

16

WHAT IS THE PRESENT TENSE?

1   The **PRESENT TENSE** indicates that the action of the verb is happening at the present time. It can be at the moment the speaker is speaking, a habitual action, or a general truth.

> I *see* you.
> He *smokes* when he *is* nervous.
> The sun *rises* every day.

IN ENGLISH

There are three verb forms that indicate the present tense. Each form has a slightly different meaning:

10

> Anja *studies* in the library.   **PRESENT**
> Anja *is studying* in the library.   **PRESENT PROGRESSIVE**
> Anja *does study* in the library.   **PRESENT EMPHATIC**

Depending on the way a question is worded, you will automatically choose one of the three above forms.

> Where does Anja study? She *studies* in the library.
> Where is Anja now? She *is studying* in the library.
> Does Anja study in the library? Yes, she *does* [*study* in the library].

IN GERMAN

20   Unlike English, there is only one verb form to indicate the present tense. The German present tense, **das Präsens**, is used to express the meaning of the English present, present progressive, and present emphatic tenses. The present tense in German is a simple tense formed by adding the present set endings to the stem of the verb (see *What is a Verb Conjugation?*, p. 45).

> Anja *studies* in the library.
> studiert

> Anja *is studying* in the library.
> studiert

30

> Anja *does study* in the library.
> studiert

CAREFUL — Remember that in the present tense there is no need for auxiliary verbs such as *is, do, does* in German; do not try to include them.

WHAT IS AN OBJECT?

An **OBJECT** is a noun or pronoun that receives the action of the verb   [1]
or is associated with a preposition.

> Axel *writes* a letter.
> | |
>   verb   direct
>   object

> Axel *writes* his mother a letter.
> | |
>   verb   indirect
>   object

> The boy left *with* his father.
> | |
>   preposition   object of a
>   preposition   [10]

In this chapter we will study the direct object and the indirect object.
The object of a preposition is covered in *What is a Preposition?*, p. 64.
Although we have limited the examples in this section to noun
objects, the same questions can be used to establish the function of
pronoun objects.

DIRECT OBJECT
(see also *What are Direct and Indirect Object Pronouns?*, p. 59)

IN ENGLISH

A direct object is a noun or pronoun that receives the action of   [20]
the verb directly, without a preposition between the verb and
the noun or pronoun. It answers the question *whom?* or *what?*
asked after the verb.

> Axel sees *Ingrid.*
> > Axel sees *whom?* Ingrid.
> > *Ingrid* is the direct object.

> Axel writes *a letter.*
> > Axel writes *what?* A letter.
> > *A letter* is the direct object.

There are two types of verbs: transitive and intransitive.   [30]

- **transitive verb** — a verb that takes a direct object. It is indicated by the abbreviation *v.t.* (verb transitive) in dictionaries.

> The boy *threw* the ball.
> | |
>   transitive   direct object

> She *lost* her job.
> | |
>   transitive   direct object

- **intransitive verb** — a verb that cannot take a direct object. It is indicated by the abbreviation *v.i.* (verb intransitive) in dictionaries.

Ingrid *arrives* today.
  intransitive adverb

Franz *is sleeping.*
  intransitive

Many verbs can be used both transitively, that is, with a direct object, and intransitively, without a direct object.

The students *speak* German.
  transitive   direct object

Actions *speak* louder than words.
  intransitive   adverbial phrase

CAREFUL — Some verbs that are transitive in English are intransitive in German, while other verbs that are intransitive in English are transitive in German.

IN GERMAN

As in English, a direct object is a noun or pronoun that receives the action of the verb directly. It answers the question **wen?** *(whom?)* or **was?** *(what?)* asked after the verb. Direct objects are expressed by the accusative case in German.

Niko liest **das Buch.**
  Niko reads *what?* The book.
  Das Buch is the direct object → accusative case
  *Niko reads **the book.***

A few verbs take dative case direct objects in German instead of accusative case direct objects. These are referred to as **DATIVE VERBS**. Here are two examples.

- **danken** *(to thank)*

  Sie danken **dem Polizisten.**
    They thank *whom?* The policeman (**dem Polizisten**).
    Dem Polizisten is the direct object, but in the dative case.
    *They thank **the policeman.***

- **helfen** *(to help)*

  Wir helfen **dir.**
    We are helping *whom?* You (**dir**).
    Dir is the direct object, but in the dative case.
    *We are helping **you.***

Other common dative verbs include **folgen** *(follow)*, **gefallen** *(like)*, and **glauben** *(believe)*.

Verbs whose direct objects are expressed in the dative do not also have indirect objects (see below). Your German textbook will indicate the verbs that take direct objects in the dative case, and you will need to memorize them. [80]

CAREFUL — An English verb that requires a preposition before its object (see pp. 64-5) may have an equivalent German verb that requires a direct object in the accusative.

> *She is looking **for her coat**.*
>> She is looking *for what? Her coat* is the object of the preposition *for.*
>
> Sie sucht **ihren Mantel**.
>
>> **suchen** *(to look for)* takes a direct object → **ihren mantel** → accusative case [90]

INDIRECT OBJECT
(see also *What are Direct and Indirect Object Pronouns?*, p. 59)

IN ENGLISH

An indirect object is a noun or pronoun that receives the action of the verb indirectly. It answers the question *to* or *for whom?* or *to* or *for what?* asked after the verb.

> Axel wrote *his brother* a letter.
>> He wrote a letter *to whom?* His brother.
>> *His brother* is the indirect object. [100]
>
> Axel did *his brother* a favor.
>> He did a favor *for whom?* His brother.
>> *His brother* is the indirect object.

Sometimes the word *to* is included in the English sentence.

> Axel spoke *to Lukas and Ingrid.*
>> Axel spoke *to whom?* To Lukas and Ingrid.
>> *Lukas* and *Ingrid* are two indirect objects.

IN GERMAN

As in English, an indirect object is a noun or pronoun that receives the action of the verb indirectly. It answers the question **wem?** *(to or for whom?)* or **was?** *(to or for what?)* asked after the verb. Indirect objects are expressed by the dative case in German. [110]

> Niko schreibt **seinem Bruder**.
>> Niko writes a letter *to whom?* His brother.
>> **Seinem Bruder** is the indirect object → dative case
> *Niko writes **(to) his brother**.*
>
> Ingrid tat **mir** einen Gefallen.
>> Ingrid did a favor *for whom?* Me. [120]
>> **Mir** is the indirect object → dative case
> *Ingrid did **me** a favor.*

SENTENCES WITH A DIRECT AND AN INDIRECT OBJECT

A sentence may contain both a direct object and an indirect object, either as nouns or pronouns.

IN ENGLISH

When a sentence has both a direct and an indirect object, two word orders are possible, one without "to" preceding the indirect object and one with the preposition "to".

- If the indirect object is not preceded by "to," the word order is as follows: subject (S) + verb (V) + indirect object (IO) + direct object (DO).

    Johan gave his sister a gift.
        S   V   IO   DO

    Who gave a gift? Johan.
    Johan is the subject.

    Johan gave a gift *to whom?* His sister.
    His sister is the indirect object.

    Johan gave *what?* A gift.
    A gift is the direct object.

- If the indirect object is preceded by "to," the word order is as follows: subject + verb + direct object + *to* + indirect object.

    Johan gave a gift to his sister.
        S   V   DO *to*   IO

The first structure without "to" is the most common. However, since there is no "to" preceding the indirect object *(sister)*, it is more difficult to identify its function than in the second structure.

IN GERMAN

As in English, a sentence can have both a direct and an indirect object. The order of the objects in the German sentence depends on whether they are nouns or pronouns and on their function. For example:

- noun objects → indirect object + direct object
- pronoun objects → direct object + indirect object
- pronoun and noun objects → pronoun + noun

The order of the objects can also depend on a particular word you want to emphasize. Consult your textbook for details.

WHAT ARE DIRECT AND INDIRECT OBJECT PRONOUNS?

An **OBJECT PRONOUN** is a pronoun used as an direct or indirect   1
object.

> Axel saw *us*.
>> Axel saw *whom?* Us.
>> Pronoun *us* → direct object of *saw*
>
> My parents wrote *me* a letter.
>> My parents wrote a letter *to whom?* Me.
>> Pronoun *me* → indirect object of *wrote*

The various functions of object pronouns are established in the same
way as the function of object nouns (see *What is an Object?*, p. 55).

IN ENGLISH   10

Most pronouns used as direct and indirect objects in English are
different in form from the ones used as subjects (see *What is a
Subject Pronoun?*, p. 41).

	SUBJECT NOMINATIVE	**OBJECT** OBJECTIVE
SINGULAR		
1ˢᵗ PERSON	I	me
2ᴺᴰ PERSON	you	you
3ᴿᴰ PERSON	he	him
	she	her
	it	it
PLURAL		
1ˢᵗ PERSON	we	us
2ᴺᴰ PERSON	you	you
3ᴿᴰ PERSON	they	them

20

Here are a few examples of the usage of nominative and objective pronouns.

> *He* and *I* work for the newspaper.
> subjects: 3ʳᵈ pers. sing. + 1ˢᵗ pers. sing.
> nominative case   30

> The politician invited *him* and *me* to lunch.
> direct objects: 3ʳᵈ pers. sing. + 1ˢᵗ pers. sing.
> objective case

> *They* took their car to the garage.
> subject: 3ʳᵈ pers. pl.
> nominative case

I lent *them* my car.

indirect object: 3ʳᵈ pers. pl.
objective case

IN GERMAN

Unlike English, which has only one objective case for pronouns, German uses two cases, the accusative and the dative. Look at the chart below.

ENGLISH		GERMAN		
OBJECTIVE		ACCUSATIVE	DATIVE	
SINGULAR				
1ˢᵗ PERSON	*me*	mich	mir	
2ᴺᴰ PERSON	*you*	{ dich	dir	FAMILIAR
		{ Sie	Ihnen	FORMAL
		{ *him*	ihn	ihm	MASCULINE
3ᴿᴰ PERSON	{ *her*	sie	ihr	FEMININE
	{ *it*	es	ihm	NEUTER
PLURAL				
1ˢᵗ PERSON	*us*	uns	uns	
2ᴺᴰ PERSON	*you*	{ euch	euch	FAMILIAR
		{ Sie	Ihnen	FORMAL
3ᴿᴰ PERSON	*them*	sie	ihnen	

Two English object pronouns have more than one equivalent in German: *you* and *it*. Let us look at these two object pronouns.

FAMILIAR "YOU" AS OBJECT PRONOUN

(see pp. 37-8 in *What is a Personal Pronoun?*)

The familiar forms of *you* can be singular or plural, depending on whether the *you* addressed is one or more persons, each form having an accusative and dative form.

- **singular** — You are speaking to one person → **dich** (acc.); **dir** (dat.)

    *We see **you**, Anna.*
    Wir sehen **dich**, Anna.

    sehen *(to see)* takes an accusative object

    *We are helping **you**, Anna.*
    Wir helfen **dir**, Anna.

    helfen *(to help)* takes a dative object

- **plural** — You are speaking to more than one person → **euch** (acc. and dat.)

We see you, Effi and Franz.
Wir sehen **euch**, Effi und Franz.

sehen *(to see)* takes an accusative object

We are helping you, Effi and Franz.
Wir helfen **euch**, Effi und Franz.

helfen *(to help)* takes a dative object

FORMAL "YOU" AS OBJECT PRONOUN
(see p. 38 in *What is a Personal Pronoun?*)

The formal form of *you* has two forms, the accusative and the dative; the same form is used for the singular and the plural.

- **accusative** — You are speaking to one or more persons → **Sie** (acc. sing. and pl.)

    We will see you tomorrow, Mrs. Erb.
    Wir sehen **Sie** morgen, Frau Erb.

    sehen *(to see)* takes an accusative object

- **dative** — You are speaking to one or more persons → **Ihnen** (dat. sing. and pl.)

    We are glad to help you, Dr. Fried.
    Wir helfen **Ihnen** gern, Dr. Fried.

    helfen *(to help)* takes a dative object

"IT" AS OBJECT PRONOUN

German has six different object pronouns equivalent to *it*, depending on the gender of the antecedent and the case of the pronoun (accusative or dative).

To choose the correct form, follow these steps:

1. ANTECEDENT: Find the noun *it* replaces.
2. GENDER: Determine the gender of the antecedent.
3. FUNCTION: Determine the function of *it* in the sentence.
4. CASE: Choose the case that corresponds to the function.
5. SELECTION: Select the form, depending on steps 2 and 4.

Let us look at some examples.

- masculine antecedent → **ihn** (accusative) or **ihm** (dative)

    Did you see the film? Yes, I saw it.
    ANTECEDENT: the film
    GENDER: **der Film** *(the film)* → masculine
    FUNCTION: direct object of *see* **(sehen)**
    CASE: accusative
    SELECTION: masculine accusative → **ihn**

    Hast du den Film gesehen? Ja, ich habe **ihn** gesehen.

- feminine antecedent → **sie** (acc.) or **ihr** (dat.)

Are you reading the newspaper? Yes, I am reading it.
    ANTECEDENT: the newspaper
    GENDER: **die Zeitung** *(the newspaper)* → feminine
    FUNCTION: direct object of *read* **(lesen)**
    CASE: accusative
    SELECTION: feminine accusative → **sie**
Lesen Sie die Zeitung? Ja, ich lese **sie.**

- neuter antecedent → **es** (acc.) or **ihm** (dat.)

Do you understand the book? Yes, I understand it.
    ANTECEDENT: the book
    GENDER: **das Buch** *(the book)* → neuter
    FUNCTION: direct object of *understand* **(verstehen)**
    CASE: accusative
    SELECTION: neuter accusative → **es**
Verstehen Sie das Buch? Ja, ich verstehe **es.**

CAREFUL — In English you use the objective pronouns *him* or *her,* depending on the sex of the person you are referring to. In German, however, since the gender of the pronoun is based on the grammatical gender, not the sex, of the noun being replaced, a neuter noun is replaced by a neuter pronoun, **es** (accusative) or **ihm** (dative). This is the case of neuter nouns such as **das Kind** *(the child)* and nouns ending with the neuter diminutives -**chen** or -**lein**, such as **das Mädchen** *(the young girl)* or **das Fräulein** *(the young woman)*, see p. 19.

Who helps the child? We are helping her (or him).
    ANTECEDENT: the child
    GENDER: **das Kind** *(the child)* → neuter
    FUNCTION: object of *help* (**helfen** takes a dative object)
    CASE: dative
    SELECTION: neuter dative → **ihm**
Wer hilft dem Kind? Wir helfen **ihm.**
                                        |
                              dative object

██████ **STUDY TIPS — DIRECT AND INDIRECT OBJECT PRONOUNS** ██████

Flashcard
On the personal pronoun flashcards (see p. 39), add sentences illustrating the pronoun's direct and indirect object forms. Underline the object pronouns; this will draw your attention to form changes, depending on the pronoun's function in the sentence.

er	*he, it* (subject)
Ich sehe <u>ihn</u>.	*I see him/it.* (direct object)
Ich gebe <u>ihm</u> das Buch.	*I give him the book.* (indirect object)

sie	*they* (subject)
Ich sehe <u>sie</u>.	*I see them.* (direct object)
Ich gebe <u>ihnen</u> das Buch.	*I give them the book.* (indirect object)

Pattern

1. Look for similarities between direct object pronouns (accusative) and other parts of speech. Refer to the chart on p. 60.

   What pattern do you see?
   - 1st and 2nd pers. sing. (**mich, dich**) the same initial letters (**m-, d-**) as possessive adjectives (**mein, dein**), chart p. 112
   - 2nd pers. formal (**Sie**) and 3rd pers. pl. (**sie**) the same as subject pronoun, chart pp. 41-2
   - 3rd pers. sing. and pl. pronoun (**-n, -e, -s; e**) the same last letter as definite articles for direct objects (**den, die, das; die**), chart p. 31-2

2. Look for similarities between direct object pronouns (accusative) and indirect object pronouns (dative), as well as other parts of speech.

   What pattern do you see?
   - 1st and 2nd pers. informal sing. (**mir, dir**): direct object ending –ch (**mich, dich**) changes to **–r** in indirect object
   - 1st and 2nd pers. informal pl. (**uns, euch**): same forms for direct and indirect object pronouns
   - 2nd pers. formal (**Sie, Sie, Ihnen**) and 3rd pers. plural (**sie, sie, ihnen**): same forms for subject, direct, and indirect pronouns, except for capitalization.
   - 3rd pers. sing. and pl . indirect object pronoun last letter (**-m, -r, -m; n**): same as definite articles for indirect objects (**dem, der, dem; den**)

Practice

1. Write a series of short German sentences with masculine, feminine, neuter, and plural direct objects. Rewrite the sentences replacing the direct object with the appropriate object pronoun.

Ich kaufe die Blumen.	*I buy the flowers.*
Ich kaufe sie.	*I buy them.*

2. Add an indirect object to the original sentences you created under 1 above. Rewrite the sentences replacing the indirect object with the appropriate object pronoun.

Ich kaufe meiner Mutter die Blumen.	*I buy my mother flowers.*
Ich kaufe ihr die Blumen.	*I buy her flowers.*

3. Replace both the direct and indirect objects with pronouns in the sentences you've created under 2. Refer to your textbook for the correct word order.

Ich kaufe sie ihr.	*I buy them for her.*

CHAPTER

19

WHAT IS A PREPOSITION?

A **PREPOSITION** is a word usually placed in front of a noun or pronoun showing the relationship between that noun or pronoun and other words in the sentence. The noun or pronoun following the preposition is called the **OBJECT OF THE PREPOSITION**. The preposition plus its object is called a **PREPOSITIONAL PHRASE**.

prepositional phrase

Jade has an appointment *after* school.

noun   preposition   object of preposition

IN ENGLISH

Prepositions normally indicate location, direction, time, or manner.

- prepositions showing location or position

  Axel was *in* the car.
  Anna is sitting *behind* you.

- prepositions showing direction

  We went *to* school.
  The students came directly *from* class.

- prepositions showing time and date

  Many Germans go on vacation *in* August.
  Their son will be home *at* Christmas.
  I'm meeting him *before* 4:30 today.

- prepositions showing manner

  He writes *with* a pen.
  They left *without* us.

Other frequently used prepositions are: *during, since, between, of, about*. Some English prepositions are made up of more than a single word: *because of, in front of, instead of, due to, in spite of, on account of*.

An object of a preposition is a noun or pronoun that follows a preposition and is related to it. It answers the question *whom?* or *what?* asked after the preposition.

Franz is leaving without Effi.

Franz is leaving *without whom?* Without Effi.
Effi is the noun object of the preposition *without*.

The baby eats with a spoon.

The baby eats *with what?* With a spoon.
A spoon is the noun object of the preposition *with*.

When the object of the preposition is a pronoun, an object pronoun is used (see *What is an Object of Preposition Pronoun?*, p. 69).   40

> Johan goes out with her.
>> Johan goes out *with whom?* With her.
>> *Her* is the pronoun object of the preposition *with*.

IN GERMAN

Unlike in English, where the form of the noun or pronoun
object is the same regardless of the preposition, in German the
noun or pronoun object will be in the accusative, dative, or
genitive case depending on the preposition. Be sure to learn
the meaning and use of each German preposition, as well as
the case that must follow it.   50

Below are examples of various prepositions, each requiring a
different case.

- **durch** *(through)* → accusative object

> Er wirft den Ball **durch** das Fenster.
>> accusative
> *He throws the ball **through** the window.*

- **bei** *(with)* → dative object

> Er wohnt **bei** seiner Tante.
>> dative   60
> *He lives **with** his aunt.*

- **trotz** *(in spite of)* → genitive object

> **Trotz** des Regens machten wir einen Spaziergang.
>> genitive
> *In spite of the rain we took a walk.*

CAREFUL — Remember that English and German do not always
use the same preposition, or any preposition at all in the same
circumstances, and that some prepositions have multiple
meanings.   70

TWO-WAY PREPOSITIONS

German also has a group of prepositions called TWO-WAY PREPO-
SITIONS, so called because they can be followed by either an
accusative or a dative object depending on whether the preposition is used to indicate destination or location.

- when used with a verb expressing motion in a particular
  direction or from one position to another → accusative

> *We are driving **into** town tomorrow.*
>> Driving in a particular direction → accusative   80
> Wir fahren morgen **in** die Stadt.
>> accusative object

*He lays the book **on** the table.*
Book moved from one position to another → accusative
Er legt das Buch **auf** den Tisch.
accusative object

■ when used with a verb expressing location or destination →
dative

*Do you live **in** the city?*
Expressing location, no motion → dative
Wohnt ihr **in** der Stadt?
dative object

*The book lies **on** the table.*
Expressing location, no motion → dative
Das Buch liegt **auf** dem Tisch.
dative object

Note that only the prepositions belonging to the group known
as two-way prepositions take a different case to distinguish
between motion and location. All other prepositions take one
case only regardless of movement.

POSITION OF A PREPOSITION AND ITS OBJECT
IN ENGLISH
In spoken English one often encounters DANGLING PREPOSITIONS
referring to prepositions separated from their object, in particular in questions starting with *who, what, when*, etc. and in relative clauses (see p. 144). Restructuring the questions and sentences so that the preposition is placed before its object, as in
formal English, will help you identify prepositional phrases.

SPOKEN ENGLISH   →   FORMAL ENGLISH
Who did you get the book *from?*   *From whom* did you get the book?
object (*whom*)   dangling preposition   object of preposition *from*

IN GERMAN
There are no dangling prepositions. Nearly all German prepositions are placed as they are in formal English, that is, either
before their object within the sentence or at the beginning of a
question.

***Who** are you leaving **with?** →*
***With whom** are you leaving?*
Mit wem gehst du?
preposition + object

***Who** did you get the book **from?** →*
***From whom** did you get the book?*
Von wem hast du das Buch bekommen?
preposition + object

Your textbook will indicate the few prepositions that must or can follow their objects, such as **entlang: die Straße entlang** *(along the street).*

The position of prepositions in German sentences enables us to distinguish them from separable prefixes (see *What are Prefixes and Suffixes?*, p. 11). For instance, when **mit, vor,** and **an** are not placed next to their object, they are the separable prefixes of the verbs **mitkommen** *(to come along),* **vorkommen** *(to happen),* and **anhalten** *(to stop).*

> Wer **kommt mit**?
> *Who is **coming along**?*
>
> Das **kommt** manchmal **vor**.
> *That **happens** sometimes.*
>
> Der Zug **hält** in München **an**.
> *The train **stops** in Munich.*

CAREFUL — Prepositions are tricky, because every language uses prepositions differently. Do not assume that the same preposition is used in German as in English, or even that a preposition will be needed in German when you must use one in English and vice versa.

ENGLISH	GERMAN
PREPOSITION	NO PREPOSITION
to look *for*	suchen
to look *at*	betrachten
NO PREPOSITION	PREPOSITION
to answer	antworten **auf**

CHANGE OF PREPOSITION	
to protect *from*	schützen **vor** *(before)*
to wait *for*	warten **auf** *(on)*
to die *of*	sterben **an** *(at)*
to be interested *in*	interessieren *für (for)*

Do not translate an English verb + preposition word-for-word. For example, when you consult the dictionary to find the German equivalent of *to talk about*, do not stop at the first entry for *talk* (**sprechen**) and then add the German equivalent of the preposition *about*. Continue searching for the specific meaning *talk about*, which corresponds to the verb **sprechen** with the preposition **über** (meaning *over* or *above*).

> *We are talking **about** politics.*
> Wir sprechen **über** Politik.

On the other hand, when looking up a verb such as *to pay for something*, notice that the German equivalent **bezahlen** is used without a preposition.

We paid for the meal.
Wir **bezahlten** das Essen.

Your German textbook will introduce phrases like **warten auf** + accusative object *(to wait for)* and **bitten um** + accusative object *(to ask for)*. Make sure you learn the verb together with the preposition and its case so that you can use the entire pattern correctly.

STUDY TIPS — PREPOSITIONS

Flashcards

1. Create a card for each preposition. On the German side, include the case (Acc., Dat., Acc./Dat., or Gen.) that follows that preposition. Add a sample sentence.

2. Sort the cards according to the case that follows. To remember the case, here are some strategies other learners have used:

    a) Preposition + accusative — Create a phrase or acronym based on the first letter of each preposition in the group: **bis, für, durch,gegen, um, ohne** "Barking, furry dogs greet us often" or the acronym "dogfub."

    b) Preposition + dative — Sing the prepositions **aus, außer, bei, mit, nach, seit, von, zu** to a familiar tune. For ex.: in alphabetical order to the tune of the *Blue Danube Waltz*.

    c) Two-way prepositions — Two suggestions:

    - Imagine all the places a house-fly could fly or land in relation to an object, such as a wine glass: **über** *(above)*, **unter** *(below)*, **vor** *(in front of)*, **hinter** *(behind)*, **auf** *(on top of)*, **an** *(up against)*, **in** *(in)*, **neben** *(beside)*, **zwischen** *(between)*.

    - Draw two related pictures. In the first picture, illustrate an object or person moving to a new location *(The cat crawls under a chair.)*. In the second picture, illustrate that object or person in a stationary position *(The cat is sleeping under the chair.)* Under each picture, write the corresponding sentence in German using the correct preposition and case to describe the scene.

WHAT IS AN OBJECT OF PREPOSITION PRONOUN?

An **OBJECT OF PREPOSITION PRONOUN** is a pronoun used an object of   1
preposition.

> They went out with *me*.
>
> pronoun *me* object of preposition *with*

IN ENGLISH

Object of preposition pronouns are the same as the pronouns
used as direct and indirect objects. They can replace any noun
object, including persons, things, or ideas (see *What are Direct and
Indirect Object Pronouns?*, p. 59).

> The teacher saw *me*.   10
>
> direct object
>
> The teacher gave *me* the book.
>
> indirect object
>
> The teacher spoke with *me* after class.
>
> object of preposition *with*
>
> The teacher talked about *it* in class.
>
> object of preposition *about*

IN GERMAN

The objects of prepositions can be in the accusative, dative, or   20
genitive case. Normally we replace a noun object with a pronoun only if the noun replaced refers to a person. A different
construction is used when the pronoun refers to a thing or idea.
Let us look at the two types of constructions.

REFERRING TO A PERSON

When the pronoun object of a preposition refers to a person or
an animal, follow the steps you have already learned in order to
choose the appropriate personal pronoun (see p. 37).

1. ANTECEDENT — Find the noun replaced.   30
2. GENDER — Determine the gender of the antecedent.
3. CASE — Identify the case required by the preposition.
4. SELECTION — Select the appropriate pronoun form from the
   chart on p. 60.

Below are examples showing how to analyze sentences that have
a pronoun referring to a person as the object of a preposition.

Is Anja buying something for her brother?
Yes, she is buying something for him.
> 1. ANTECEDENT: brother
> 2. GENDER: **der Bruder** *(brother)* is masculine.
> 3. CASE: **für** takes an accusative object
> 4. SELECTION: masculine accusative → **ihn**

Kauft Anja etwas für ihren Bruder?
Ja, sie kauft etwas **für ihn**.

Did Franz talk about his sister?
No, he did not talk about her.
> 1. ANTECEDENT: sister
> 2. GENDER: **die Schwester** *(sister)* is feminine.
> 3. CASE: **von** takes a dative object
> 4. SELECTION: feminine dative → **ihr**

Sprach Franz von seiner Schwester?
Nein, er sprach nicht **von ihr**.

REFERRING TO A THING

To replace a pronoun object of a preposition whose antecedent is a thing or idea, German uses a construction called the **DA-COMPOUND**. It is formed by adding the prefix **da-** to the preposition, or **dar-** if the preposition begins with a vowel.

Let us look at some examples.:

> *Does Beth talk about her courses? Yes, she does talk about them.*
> Spricht Beth **von ihren Kursen**? Ja, sie spricht **davon**.
>
> preposition   noun   da-construction:
> (a thing)   **da-** + preposition **von**

> *Are you thinking about the price? Don't think about it.*
> Denken Sie **an den Preis**? Denken Sie nicht **daran**!
>
> preposition   noun   da-construction:
> (a thing)   **da-** + **-r-** + preposition **an**

These **da**-compounds are not formed with every preposition. Your German textbook will discuss this construction and its use in greater detail.

CAREFUL — Be sure to look at an entire sentence, not just at the word itself, to establish its function. For example, **ihn** *(him)* could be the direct object form (accusative) of the masculine pronoun or the object of a preposition that takes the accusative case.

STUDY TIPS — OBJECT OF PREPOSITION PRONOUNS

Pattern
Let's compare **da-** to **wo**-compounds (see *What is an Interrogative Pronoun?*, p. 118) to find similarities in form and usage.

Compare forms

wo-compound	da-compound
woran	daran
worin	darin
wofür	dafür
womit	damit

80

Compare usage

Both used when anticipating or referring to a thing or an idea, not a person.

wo-compound **in questions**	**da-compound** **in statement**
Worauf wartest du?	
Wartest du **auf den Bus**?	Nein, **darauf** warte ich nicht.
*What are you waiting **for**?*	
*Are you waiting **for the bus**?*	*No, I'm not waiting **for it**.*

CHAPTER

21

WHAT ARE THE PRINCIPAL PARTS
OF A VERB?

The principal parts of a verb are the forms needed in order to create all the different tenses.

PRESENT	I eat
PRESENT PERFECT	I have eaten
PAST	I ate
PAST PERFECT	I had eaten
FUTURE	I will eat
FUTURE PERFECT	I will have eaten

IN ENGLISH

The principal parts of an English verb are the infinitive *(to eat)*, the past tense *(ate),* and the past participle *(eaten).* If you know these parts, you can form all the other tenses of a verb (see *What is Meant by Tense?*, p. 52; *What is the Past Tense?*, p. 87; and *What is a Participle?*, p. 90).

English verbs fall into two categories, depending on how they form their principal parts.

Regular verbs — These verbs are called regular because their past tense and past participle forms follow the predictable pattern of adding *-ed*, *-d*, or *-t* to the infinitive. They have two distinct principal parts: the infinitive and the past tense.

INFINITIVE	PAST TENSE/PAST PARTICIPLE
to walk	walk*ed*
to live	live*d*
to burn	burn*ed* (burn*t*)

Irregular verbs — These verbs are called irregular because their principal parts do not follow a regular pattern. They have three distinct principal parts: the infinitive, the past tense, and the past participle.

INFINITIVE	PAST TENSE	PAST PARTICIPLE
to sing	sang	sung
to draw	drew	drawn
to hit	hit	hit
to lie	lay	lain
to ride	rode	ridden

IN GERMAN

While English makes a distinction between regular and irregular verbs, German refers to a distinction between weak verbs and strong verbs depending on how they form their principal parts (see pp. 46-7 in *What is a Verb Conjugation?*).

WEAK (REGULAR) VERBS

Weak verbs resemble English regular verbs in that the stem of the principal parts of the verb doesn't change. They have three principal parts: the infinitive, the past tense given in the 3rd person singular, and the past participle.

1st PRINCIPAL PART: INFINITIVE	kochen	*to cook*
2nd PRINCIPAL PART: PAST TENSE (3rd pers. sing.)	kochte	*cooked*
3rd PRINCIPAL PART: PAST PARTICIPLE	gekocht	*cooked*

The various principal parts are formed by adding various prefixes and/or suffixes to the stem (see *What are Prefixes and Suffixes?*, p. 11).

- the past tense is formed by adding a -t- (or -et- if the verb stem ends in -d or -t) to the stem of the infinitive + the endings for the different persons.
- the past participle is usually formed by adding the prefix **ge-** and the suffix -t or -et to the stem of the infinitive.

	INFINITIVE	PAST TENSE	PAST PARTICIPLE
to make	machen	machte	gemacht
to work	arbeiten	arbeitete	gearbeitet

STRONG (IRREGULAR) VERBS

Strong verbs resemble English irregular verbs in that they have unpredictable principal parts. They have three principal parts: the infinitive, the past tense given in the 3rd person singular, and the past participle.

1st PRINCIPAL PART: INFINITIVE	finden	*to find*
2nd PRINCIPAL PART: PAST TENSE (3rd pers. sing.)	fand	*found*
3rd PRINCIPAL PART: PAST PARTICIPLE	gefunden	*found*

The irregularity of strong verbs is shown in a variety of ways:

- the vowel of the verb stem often changes in the past tense and in the past participle.
- the past tense endings are different than those for weak verbs.
- the past participle is usually formed by adding the prefix **ge-** and the ending -en or -n.

	1ˢᵀ	2ᴺᴰ	3ᴿᴰ
	INFINITIVE	PAST TENSE	PAST PARTICIPLE
to come	kommen	kam	**gekommen**
to do	tun	tat	**getan**

Besides the irregularities listed above, other strong verbs show their irregularity in different ways:

Stem-changing verbs — These verbs have a fourth principal part: the 3ʳᵈ person singular of the present tense reflecting the stem vowel change in the 2ⁿᵈ and 3ʳᵈ person singular of the present tense.

1ˢᵗ PRINCIPAL PART: INFINITIVE	laufen	*to run*
2ⁿᵈ PRINCIPAL PART: PAST TENSE (3ʳᵈ pers. sing.)	lief	*ran*
3ʳᵈ PRINCIPAL PART: PAST PARTICIPLE	gelaufen	*run*
4ᵗʰ PRINCIPAL PART: PRESENT TENSE (3ʳᵈ pers. sing.)	läuft	*runs*

Here are a couple of examples of the four principal parts of stem-changing verbs.

	1ˢᵀ	2ᴺᴰ	3ᴿᴰ	4ᵀᴴ
	INFINITIVE	PAST TENSE	PAST PARTICIPLE	PRESENT TENSE
to read	lesen	las	**gelesen**	liest
to take	nehmen	nahm	**genommen**	nimmt

Mixed-verbs — Your German textbook will show you how to form the principal parts of these verbs which have forms that follow the weak pattern and others the strong pattern. There are not many of them, but many are very common verbs. For example, **bringen** *(to bring)*, **denken***(to think)*, **kennen** *(to know someone)*, and **wissen** *(to know something)*.

Most German dictionaries include an alphabetized list of irregular verbs with their principal parts. By memorizing the principal parts of verbs you will be able conjugate verbs properly in all their tenses.

STUDY TIPS — PRINCIPAL PARTS OF A VERB

Pattern
When you learn a new strong verb, look for another strong verb that changes its vowels in the past tense and the past participle in the same way. Make your own lists of strong verbs according to the vowel pattern in the principal parts.

INFINITIVE	PAST TENSE	PAST PARTICIPLE
-ei-	-ie-	-ie-
schreiben *(to write)*	schrieb	geschrieben
bleiben *(to stay)*	blieb	geblieben

Infinitive	Past tense	Past Participle
-i-	**-a-**	**-u-**
finden *(to find)*	fand	gefunden
trinken *(to drink)*	trank	getrunken
-ie-	**-o-**	**-o-**
fliegen *(to fly)*	flog	geflogen
verlieren *(to lose)*	verlor	verloren

Flashcard

1. To review the principal parts of verbs, take out the flashcards you created to learn the meaning of verbs (see p. 51) and sort them into two groups: weak verbs and strong verbs. On the German side, write weak or strong and add the principal parts: infinitive, past, past participle.

(weak)	kaufen	kaufte	gekauft
(strong)	gehen	ging	gegangen

2. Work with your flashcards in two ways:

   a. Group the strong verbs according to the vowel patterns you determined above. Practice saying the pattern out loud for each verb in the group. Repeat the pattern until you can remember it without looking at the card.

   b. Mix the strong and weak verbs together and go through the cards. As you practice forming the past participle, identify the verb as a weak or strong verb.
   - if weak, you need **–t** in the past participle.
   - if strong, you need **-en** in the past participle.
   - if strong, focus on the vowel pattern.
   - if there is a prefix, determine if it is separable or inseparable.
   - if separable, insert **–ge-** between the prefix and the stem.
   - if inseparable, no **ge-** is used.

CHAPTER

22

WHAT IS AN AUXILIARY VERB?

A verb is called an AUXILIARY VERB or HELPING VERB when it helps another verb, called the MAIN VERB, to form one of its tenses or alter its meaning.

He *has been gone* two weeks.   *has*   AUXILIARY VERB
                                     been   AUXILIARY VERB
                                       gone   MAIN VERB

A verb tense composed of an auxiliary verb + a main verb is called a COMPOUND TENSE. In a compound tense only the auxiliary verb is conjugated.

Julia *had studied* for the exam.

    auxiliary   main
    verb   verb
   compound tense

Julia *studies* for the exam.

    simple tense

IN ENGLISH

There are three auxiliary verbs: *to have, to be,* and *to do.*

- auxiliary verbs are used to indicate the tense of the main verb.

Jade *is reading* a book.

auxiliary *to be* + present participle of *to read*
present progressive (p. 54)

Jade *has written* a book.

auxiliary *to have* + past participle of *to write*
present perfect (p. 95)

Jade *does write* a book.

auxiliary *to do* + infinitive
present emphatic (p. 54)

- the auxiliary verb *to do* is used to help formulate questions and to make sentences negative (see *What are Declarative and Interrogative Sentences?*, p. 133 and *What are Affirmative and Negative Sentences?*, p. 130).

Does Jade *read* a book?
Jade *does not read* a book.

- the auxiliary verb *to be* is also used to indicate the verb is in the passive voice (see *What is Meant by Active and Passive Voice?*, p. 159).

The book *is read* by many people.

Modals — There is also a series of auxiliary verbs, called **MODALS,** such as *will, would, may, must, can, could,* that are used to change the tense or meaning of the main verb expressed in its infinitive form.

- the modal *will* is used to indicate the future tense.

    Jade *will read* a book.

    modal *will* + infinitive *read*

- most modals are used to change the meaning of the main verb expressed in its infinitive form.

    Jade *may read* a book.
    Jade *must read* a book.
    Jade *can read* a book.

IN GERMAN

As in English, German has auxiliary verbs and modals.

Auxiliary Verbs — The three main auxiliary verbs are **sein** *(to be)*, **haben** *(to have)*, and **werden** *(to become)*. As in English, auxiliary verbs are primarily used to indicate the tense of the main verb. In the examples below, notice that the conjugated auxiliary verb is in the second position of the sentence and the past participle or the infinitive form of the main verb is at the end of the sentence (see *What is a Participle?*, p. 90 and p. 25 in *What is a Verb?*).

- **sein** + past participle or **haben** + past participle → past tense (see *What is the Past Tense?*, p. 87)

    Franz **hat** das Buch **gelesen.**

    auxiliary **haben** + past participle of **lesen** *(to read)* → present perfect
    *Franz **read** the book. [Franz **has read** the book.]*

    Franz **ist** zur Bibliothek **gegangen.**

    auxiliary **sein** + past participle of **gehen** *(to go)* → present perfect
    *Franz **went** to the library. [Franz **has gone** to the library.]*

- **werden** + infinitive → future (see *What is the Future Tense?*, p. 85)

    Franz **wird** das Buch **lesen.**

    auxiliary **werden** + infinitive of **lesen**
    *Franz **will read** the book.*

- **werden** + past participle → passive voice

    Das Buch **wird gelesen.**

    auxiliary **werden** + past participle of **lesen** → present passive voice
    *The book **is being read.***

MODALS — As in English, German has a series of modals that are used to change the tense or meaning of the main verb expressed in the infinitive form. German modals are verbs conjugated in the present and past tenses. The modal is in the second position of the sentence and the main verb in the infinitive form is at the end of the sentence.

- **können** *(to be able, can)*
  Lukas **kann** dieses Buch **lesen.**
  *Lukas **can read** this book.*
  ₉₀ [Lukas *has the ability to read* the book.]

- **dürfen** *(to be permitted to, may)*
  Lukas **darf** dieses Buch **lesen.**
  *Lukas **may read** this book.*
  [Lukas *is allowed to read* the book.]

- **müssen** *(to be obligated to, must)*
  Lukas **muss** dieses Buch **lesen.**
  *Lukas **must read** this book.*
  [Lukas *has to read* the book.]

- **sollen** *(to be supposed to, should)*
  ₁₀₀ Lukas **soll** dieses Buch **lesen.**
  *Lukas **should read** this book.*
  [Lukas *ought to read* the book.]

- **wollen** *(to want to)*
  Lukas **will** dieses Buch **lesen.**
  *Lukas **wants to read** this book.*

CAREFUL — Don't confuse **will**, the 1st and 3rd person singular form of the German modal verb **wollen** *(to want)*, and the English modal *will* that puts the main verb in the future.

> Ich **will** gehen.   (**wollen** = *to want to* → MODAL)
> *I **want** to go.*

> Ich **werde** gehen.   (**werden** = *to become* → AUXILIARY TO FORM
> *I **will** go.*   FUTURE TENSE)

Consult your textbook for the meaning of German modal verbs and how they are used.

STUDY TIPS — AUXILIARY VERBS

Pattern
Compare the conjugation of modal verbs with the conjugation of regular and stem-changing verbs you learned previously.

REGULAR **wohnen** *(to live)*		STEM-CHANGING **fahren** *(to drive)*		MODAL **können** *(to be able to, can)*		MODAL **müssen** *(to have to, must)*	
wohne	wohnen	fahre	fahren	kann	können	muss	müssen
wohnst	wohnt	fährst	fahrt	kannst	könnt	musst	müsst
wohnt	wohnen	fährt	fahren	kann	können	muss	müssen

What similarities and differences do you see?

1. All verbs: 2nd per. sing. end with -st.
2. All verbs: infinitive, 1st and 3rd pers. pl. identical forms.
3. Modal verbs: 1st and 3rd pers. sing. identical.
4. Vowel change: stem-changing verbs have a vowel change in 2nd and 3rd pers. sing. vs. modal verbs have a vowel change in the 1st, 2nd, and 3rd pers. sing.
5. Endings: regular and stem-changing verbs have an ending in the 1st, 2nd, and 3rd pers. sing., vs. modal verbs have no ending in the 1st and 3rd pers. sing., only in the 2nd pers. sing.

130

Flashcards

Create a flashcard for each modal verb. On the German side, include the conjugation pattern and a sample sentence.

CHAPTER

23

WHAT ARE REFLEXIVE PRONOUNS AND VERBS?

A **REFLEXIVE VERB** is a verb that is accompanied by a pronoun, called a **REFLEXIVE PRONOUN**, that serves *to reflect* the action of the verb back to the subject.

> subject = reflexive pronoun → the same person
>
> She *cut herself* with the knife.
>   reflexive verb

IN ENGLISH

Many regular verbs can take on a reflexive meaning by adding a reflexive pronoun.

> The child *dresses* the doll.
>   regular verb
>
> The child *dresses herself.*
>   verb + reflexive pronoun

In some regional varieties of spoken English, many verbs are made reflexive with an object pronoun instead of a reflexive pronoun (see p. 59 in *What is an Object Pronoun?*).

> I'll go get *me* a glass of water.
>   object pronoun instead of reflexive pronoun *myself*

Reflexive pronouns end with *-self* in the singular and *-selves* in the plural.

	SUBJECT PRONOUN	REFLEXIVE PRONOUN
SINGULAR		
1ST PERSON	I	myself
2ND PERSON	you	yourself
3RD PERSON	he	himself
	she	herself
	it	itself
PLURAL		
1ST PERSON	we	ourselves
2ND PERSON	you	yourselves
3RD PERSON	they	themselves

As the subject changes so does the reflexive pronoun, because they both refer to the same person or object.

> I cut *myself.*
> Hans and Julia blamed *themselves* for the accident.

Although the subject pronoun *you* is the same for the singular and plural, there is a difference in the reflexive pronouns: *yourself* (singular) is used when you are speaking to one person and *yourselves* (plural) is used when you are speaking to more than one.

> *Johan,* did *you* make *yourself* a sandwich?
> *Children,* make sure *you* wash *yourselves* properly.

Reflexive verbs can be in any tense: *I wash myself* (present), *I washed myself* (past), *I will wash myself* (future), etc. Reflexive pronouns can function as either direct objects, indirect objects, or objects of a preposition, but the form is the same regardless of the function (see *What is an Object?*, p. 55 and *What is a Preposition?*, p. 64).

IN GERMAN

REFLEXIVE PRONOUNS

As in English, there is a different reflexive pronoun for each person. Since the reflexive pronoun can function as a direct object, indirect object, or object of a preposition, German reflexive pronouns have an accusative and dative form. As you can see in the chart below, the same form is used for accusative and dative reflexive pronouns, except for the 1st and 2nd persons singular.

SUBJECT	REFLEXIVE		
NOMINATIVE	ACCUSATIVE	DATIVE	
ich	mich	mir	*myself*
du	dich	dir	*yourself*
er			
sie }	sich	sich	*himself, herself,*
es			*itself*
wir	uns	uns	*ourselves*
ihr	euch	euch	*yourselves*
sie	sich	sich	*themselves*
Sie	sich	sich	*yourself, yourselves*

Here are a few sentences illustrating the use of the accusative or dative reflexive pronoun, depending on its function, the verb and the preposition.

- as direct or indirect object of the verb

> *I cut **myself** with the knife.*
>
>   direct object of *cut*
>
> Ich habe **mich** mit dem Messer geschnitten.
>
>   accusative object of **geschnitten** *(to cut)*

*You should write **yourself** a note.*
　　　　　　|
　　　　indirect object of *write*
　　　　You should write *to whom*? To yourself → indirect object

Du solltest **dir** einen Zettel schreiben.
　　　　　　|
　　dative object of **schreiben** *(to write)*

- as object of a preposition

*He thinks only of **himself**.*
　　　　　　|
　　object of preposition *of*
　　to think of → **denken an** + accusative

Er denkt nur an **sich**.
　　　　　|
　　accusative object of **denken an**

*You talk about **yourself** too much.*
　　　　　|
　　object of preposition *about*
　　to talk about → **reden von** + dative

Du redest zuviel von **dir**.
　　　　　|
　　dative object of **von**

REFLEXIVE VERBS

Unlike English where the meaning of a regular verb can be changed by adding a reflexive pronoun, German has a series of verbs, called **REFLEXIVE VERBS,** whose meaning can only be conveyed with a reflexive pronoun. The English equivalents of these verbs do not have reflexive pronouns. Reflexive verbs are listed in the dictionary with the 3ʳᵈ person reflexive pronoun **sich** + the infinitive.

sich erholen	*to recover*
sich befinden	*to be located*
sich verlieben	*to fall in love*

As in English, German reflexive verbs are conjugated in the various persons followed by a reflexive pronoun. Look at the conjugation of **sich erholen** *(to recover)* that takes an accusative object.

SINGULAR

1ˢᵗ PERSON	ich erhole mich	*I recover*
2ⁿᵈ PERSON FAMILIAR	du erholst dich	*you recover*
3ʳᵈ PERSON	er erholt sich	*he, it recovers*
	sie erholt sich	*she, it recovers*
	es erholt sich	*it recovers*

PLURAL

1ˢᵗ PERSON	wir erholen uns	*we recover*
2ⁿᵈ PERSON FAMILIAR	ihr erholt euch	*you recover*
3ʳᵈ PERSON	sie erholen sich	*they recover*
2ⁿᵈ PERSON FORMAL	Sie erholen sich	*you recover*

As in English, reflexive verbs can be conjugated in all tenses. The subject pronoun and reflexive pronoun remain the same; only the verb form changes: *du* **erholst** *dich* (present), *du* **wirst** *dich* **erholen** (future), *du* **hast** *dich* **erholt** (perfect).

As you learn new vocabulary, you will need to memorize which German verbs require a reflexive pronoun as part of the whole verb, the ones that can be used with or without a reflexive pronoun, and the ones that have a different meaning when they are reflexive. Remember that the German reflexive pronouns are not always translated in the English sentence. Your German textbook will introduce you to the various types of verbs and their English equivalent.

130

CAREFUL — Pay special attention to verbs that take a direct object in English but require the dative case in German. These so-called dative verbs take a reflexive pronoun in the dative case (see pp. 56-7 in *What is an Object?*.

140

>*I can't help **myself**.*
>direct object of *help*
>Remember: *to help* → **helfen** + dative
>Ich kann **mir** nicht helfen.
>dative object of **helfen**

RECIPROCAL ACTION

IN ENGLISH

English uses a regular verb followed by the expression "each other" to express reciprocal action, that is, an action between two or more persons or things.

150

>The dog and the cat looked at *each other*.
>The expression "each other" tells us that the action of *looking* was reciprocal, i.e., the dog looked at the cat and the cat looked at the dog.

>Our children call *each other* every day.
>The expression "each other" tells us that the action of *calling* is reciprocal, i.e., the various children call one another every day.

Since reciprocal verbs require that more than one person or thing be involved, the verb is always plural.

IN GERMAN

German uses reflexive pronouns to express an action that is reciprocal.

160

>Wir **sehen uns** morgen.
>*We'll **see each other** tomorrow.*

>Unsere Kinder **rufen sich** jeden Tag an.
>*Our children **call each other** every day.*

STUDY TIPS — REFLEXIVE PRONOUNS AND VERBS

Flashcards

Create flashcards for reflexive verbs. On the German side, include **sich** and the infinitive form of the verb and indicate the case of the reflexive pronoun. Finally, write two sample sentences in the first and third person singular.

170

sich interessieren (acc.)	*to be interested* in something
	Ich interessiere mich für Schach.
	I'm interested in chess.
	Sie interessiert sich für Sport.
	She is interested in sports.

WHAT IS THE FUTURE TENSE?

The **FUTURE TENSE** indicates that the action of the verb will take place some time in the future.

> I *will return* the book as soon as I can.
> └─────┘
> future

IN ENGLISH

The future tense is formed with the auxiliary *will* or *shall* + the dictionary form of the main verb. In conversation *shall* and *will* are often shortened to *'ll*. The time the future action will occur may or may not be indicated.

> Axel *will do* his homework after supper.
> I'll take my umbrella because it will rain.

An action that will take place in the future can also be expressed in the present tense. In this case, the time the future action will occur must be indicated by an adverb or an expression implying the future (see *What is an Adverb?*, p. 140).

> Max *is meeting* Axel *tomorrow*.
> └──────────┘   └──┘
> present progressive   adverb

> Johan *goes* to Berlin *next week*.
> │   └────────┘
> present   expression of future time

IN GERMAN

The future tense, **das Futur**, is formed with the auxiliary verb **werden** *(to become)* + the infinitive of the main verb. The verb **werden** is conjugated to agree with the subject and the infinitive remains unchanged. Note the order of the verb parts: the conjugated verb is placed in the 2nd position and the infinitive is placed at the end of the sentence (see *What is a Sentence?*, p. 126).

> Lukas und Max **werden** ihre Hausaufgabe **schreiben**.
> │   │
> 3rd pers. pl.   infinitive
> *Lukas and Max **will write** their homework.*

> Ich **werde** heute Abend **ausgehen**.
> │   │
> 1st pers. sing.   infinitive
> *I **shall go out** tonight.*

As in English, an action that will take place in the future can also be expressed in the present tense with an adverb or an expression of future time.

Hans und Lukas **schreiben morgen** ihre Prüfung.

present + adverb of future time

*Hans and Lukas **are writing** their test **tomorrow**.*

Er **fliegt nächstes Jahr** nach Deutschland.

present + expression of future time

*He **is flying** to Germany **next year**.*

CAREFUL — Be sure to use the correct form of **werden** when forming the future tense in German. The verb form **will** comes from the modal verb **wollen** and does not indicate future tense (see Careful, p. 78).

FUTURE OF PROBABILITY

In addition to expressing an action that will take place in the future, the future tense in German can be used to express a probable fact, or what the speaker feels is probably true. This is called the **FUTURE OF PROBABILITY**.

IN ENGLISH

The idea of probability is expressed in the present tense accompanied with words such as *must, probably, wonder*.

My keys *must* be around here.
My keys are *probably* around here.

I *wonder* if my keys are around here.

IN GERMAN

Unlike English that uses the present tense, the idea of probability in German is usually expressed in the future tense accompanied with words such as **wohl** *(probably)*, **sicher** *(surely)*, and **vielleicht** *(perhaps)*.

Meine Schlüssel **werden wohl** irgendwo hier **liegen**.

my   keys   **will**   **probably** around here lie

adverb (**wohl**) + future tense of **liegen** *(to lie)*

*My keys **are probably** around here.*

adverb + present tense of *to be*

Sie **werden** dieses Buch **sicher kennen**.

you **will**   this   book   **surely   know**

adverb (**sicher**) + future tense of **kennen** *(to know)*

*You **surely know** this book.*

adverb + present tense of *to know*

WHAT IS THE PAST TENSE?

The **PAST TENSE** indicates that the action of the verb occurred in the past. [1]

> I *saw* you yesterday.

IN ENGLISH

There are several verb forms that indicate the past tense.

I worked	SIMPLE PAST
I was working	PAST PROGRESSIVE
I used to work	HABITUAL PAST
	(WITH HELPING VERB USED TO)
I did work	PAST EMPHATIC [10]
I have worked	PRESENT PERFECT
I had worked	PAST PERFECT

The simple past is a simple tense; that is, it consists of one word, *worked* in the example above. The other past tenses are compound tenses; that is, they consist of more than one word, an auxiliary plus a main verb, *was working, did work* in the example above (see *What is an Auxiliary Verb?*, p. 76). In spoken English, the two tenses are often interchangeable.

Simple past — There are two ways to form the simple past. If the verb is regular, the ending *–ed* (or *-d*) is added. If the verb is [20] irregular, vowel and/or consonant changes are common.

REGULAR		IRREGULAR	
work	work*ed*	sing	s*a*ng
live	live*d*	see	s*aw*

Present perfect — The present perfect is formed with the auxiliary *to have* in the present tense + the past participle of the main verb (see *What is the Present Tense?*, p. 54 and *What is a Participle?*, p. 90).

> I *have worked.* [30]
> present | past participle of *to work*

> I *have seen* that film.
> present | past participle of *to see*

IN GERMAN

There are two tenses commonly used to express an action in the past: the simple past and the present perfect.

Simple past — The simple past, **das Imperfekt** or **das Präteritum**, consists of only one word: the verb stem + the simple past ending (**-te**) or a verb stem with a change in spelling.

> Ich **wohnte** in Hannover.
> verb stem **wohn-** + ending **-te**
> *I **lived** in Hanover.*

> Ich **schwamm** jeden Tag.
> verb stem **schwamm-** (**schwimmen**, *to swim*) + no ending
> *I **swam** every day.*

The formation of the simple past depends on whether the verb is a strong or a weak verb (see pp. 46-7). Both the spelling of the verb stem and the endings may be affected. Your German textbook will explain in detail the formation of the simple past.

Present perfect — The present perfect tense, **das Perfekt**, is a compound tense, consisting of two parts: the auxiliary verbs **haben** *(to have)* or **sein** *(to be)* conjugated in the present tense + the past participle of the main verb. You must memorize which verbs require **haben** and which require **sein** as the auxiliary.

> Ich **habe** in Hannover **gewohnt.**
> present tense   past participle
> auxiliary **haben**   main verb **wohnen** *(to live)*
> *I **have lived** in Hanover. [I've **lived** in Hanover.]*

> Ich **bin** jeden Tag **geschwommen.**
> present tense   past participle of
> auxiliary **sein**   main verb **schwimmen** *(to swim)*
> *I **have swum** every day. [I've **swum** every day.]*

As in informal English, the simple past and the present perfect have equivalent meanings in German. Their difference is one of style and usage: generally, the present perfect is used in conversation, whereas the simple past is more common in certain kinds of writing. Consult your textbook for more information.

STUDY TIPS — PAST TENSE

Pattern

Compare the conjugation of weak and strong verbs in the present and the past tense.

WEAK VERB
wohnen *(to live)*

	PRESENT		PAST
Singular				80
1st	wohne	1st/3rd	wohnte
2nd	wohnst	2nd	wohntest
3rd	wohnt		
Plural			
1st/3rd	wohnen	1st/3rd	wohnten
2nd	wohnt	2nd	wohntet

STRONG VERB
fahren *(to drive)*

	PRESENT		PAST
Singular			
1st	fahre	1st/3rd	fuhr	90
2nd	fährst	2nd	fuhrst
3rd	fährt		
Plural			
1st/3rd	fahren	1st/3rd	fuhren
2nd	fahrt	2nd	fuhrt

What similarities and differences do you see?

Endings:

- all verbs and tenses: 1st and 3rd pers. pl. are the same.
- strong and weak verbs past tense: 1st and 3rd pers. sing. are the same.
- strong verbs past tense: 1st and 3rd pers. sing. no ending; other endings same as in present tense.
- weak verbs past tense: all forms insert a **-t-** or **-te-** before the ending.

Vowel change:

- weak verbs: no vowel change from present to past.
- stem-changing verbs: stem vowel change in present tense occurs only in the 2nd and 3rd pers. sing.
- strong verbs: stem vowel change in past tense occurs in all forms.

CHAPTER

26

WHAT IS A PARTICIPLE?

A **PARTICIPLE** is a form of a verb that can be used in one of two ways: with an auxiliary verb to indicate certain tenses or as an adjective to describe something.

He *has closed* the door.
auxiliary + participle → past tense

He heard me through the *closed* door.
participle describing *door* → adjective

There are two types of participles: the present participle and the past participle.

PRESENT PARTICIPLE
IN ENGLISH

The present participle is easy to recognize because it is the *-ing* form of the verb: *working, studying, dancing, playing.*

The present participle has three primary uses:

- as the main verb in compound tenses with the auxiliary verb *to be* (see *What is an Auxiliary Verb?*, p. 76)

    She *is writing* with her new pen.
    present progressive of *to write*

    They *were sleeping*.
    past progressive of *to sleep*

- as an adjective (see *What is a Descriptive Adjective?*, p. 100)

    Jade is a *loving* daughter.
    describes the noun *daughter*

    He woke the *sleeping* child.
    describes the noun *child*

- in a phrase (see p. 126)

    Turning the corner, Tony ran into a tree.
    participial phrase describing *Tony*

IN GERMAN

The present participle is always formed by adding **-d** to the infinitive (see p. 25).

INFINITIVE	PRESENT PARTICIPLE
singen	singend
spielen	spielen**d**
sprechen	sprechend

40

Unlike English where present participles are used primarily as part of the main verb and in participial phrases, in German they are mainly used as adjectives with adjective endings.

eine **liebende** Tochter
*a **loving** daughter*

das **schlafende** Kind
*the **sleeping** child*

CAREFUL — Never assume that an English word ending with 50 *-ing* is translated by its German counterpart ending in **-d**. The English progressive tenses formed with an auxiliary + present participle (she *is singing*, they *were dancing*) do not exist in German. These tenses are expressed by a one word German verb whose tense corresponds to the tense of the auxiliary.

*She **is singing**.*
   present progressive
Sie **singt**.
  present

*They **were dancing**.* 60
  past progressive
Sie **tanzten**.
  simple past

PAST PARTICIPLE
IN ENGLISH

The past participle is formed differently, depending on whether the verb is regular or irregular (see p. 46). It is the form of the verb that follows the various forms of the auxiliary *to have*: I *have spoken*, he *has written*, we *have walked*. 70

The past participle has three primary uses:

- as the main verb in perfect tenses with the auxiliary verb *to have* (see *What is the Past Tense?*, p. 87; *What is the Past Perfect Tense?*, p. 95; and *What is the Future Perfect Tense?*, p. 97)

I *have written* all that I have to say.
  present perfect of *to write*

He *had*n't *spoken* to me all day.
  past perfect of *to speak*

80

- as the main verb in the passive voice with the auxiliary verb *to be* (see *What is Meant by Active and Passive Voice?*, p. 159)

  That language *is* no longer *spoken.*

  present passive

  That book *was written* last year.

  past passive

- as an adjective

  Is the *written* word more important than the *spoken* word?

  describes the noun *word*   describes the noun *word*

IN GERMAN

The past participle is formed differently depending on whether the verb is weak or strong (see p. 46). While most weak verbs form their past participle according to the same rule, strong verbs have irregular past participles that must be memorized.

Weak verbs — The past participles of weak verbs are formed by adding the prefix **ge-** and the suffix **-t** to the stem of the infinitive (see p. 25).

INFINITIVE	STEM	PAST PARTICIPLE	
machen	mach-	**ge**mach**t**	*made*
glauben	glaub-	**ge**glaub**t**	*believed*

Strong verbs — The past participles of strong verbs often change the stem vowel, and occasionally some of the consonants. The prefix **ge-** and the ending **-en** or **-n** are usually added to the stem.

INFINITIVE	PAST PARTICIPLE	
schlafen	**ge**schlaf**en**	*slept*
gehen	**ge**gang**en**	*gone*
finden	**ge**fund**en**	*found*
liegen	**ge**leg**en**	*lain*

Weak and strong verbs with an inseparable prefix do not add the prefix **ge-** and verbs with a separable prefix add **ge-** between the prefix and the stem (see *What are Prefixes and Suffixes?*, p. 11).

INSEPARABLE	besuchen	besuchte	besucht	*to visit*
SEPARABLE	**aus**suchen	suchte...aus	aus**ge**sucht	*to choose*
INSEPARABLE	bekommen	bekam	bekommen	*to receive*
SEPARABLE	**mit**kommen	kam...mit	mit**ge**kommen	*to come along*

As in English, the past participle can be used in the perfect tenses, in the passive, and as an adjective.

- as the main verb in the perfect tenses: **haben** *(to have)* or **sein** *(to be)* + the past participle

  > Ich **habe** das Buch **gelesen**.
  > *I **have read** the book. [I **read** the book.]*
  > Ich **bin** nach Hause **gekommen**.
  > *I **have come** home. [I **came** home.]*

- as the main verb in the passive voice: **werden** *(to become)* + the past participle

  > Das Buch **wird** von vielen Studenten **gelesen**.
  > *The book **is read** by many students.*

- as an adjective with adjective endings

  > Ich lese den **getippten** Brief.
  > *I read the **typed** letter.*

Since there is no way to predict the past participle of a strong verb, you will have to memorize it when you learn the verb.

PRESENT PARTICIPLE VERSUS GERUND

A VERBAL NOUN, also called a GERUND, is the form of a verb that functions as a noun in a sentence: it can be a subject, a direct object, an indirect object, or an object of a preposition.

It is important that you learn to distinguish an English participle from a gerund since German gerunds differ in form from present participles.

IN ENGLISH

Gerund — A word ending in *-ing* is a gerund if you can use the interrogative pronoun *what* to replace it in a question. The gerund will answer this question.

> *Reading* can be fun.
> > *What* can be fun? Reading.
> > *Reading,* a noun derived from the verb *to read,*
> > is the subject of the sentence.

> We have often thought about *moving*.
> > We often thought about *what*? Moving.
> > *Moving,* a noun derived from the verb *to move,*
> > is the object of the preposition *about*.

Present participle — A word ending in *-ing* is a present participle if you must use the verb *to do* to replace it in a question. The present participle will answer this question.

> We are *reading*.
> > What *are we doing*? Reading.
> > *Reading,* the present participle of the verb *to read,*
> > is part of the compound verb tense.

130

140

150

160

The family is *moving* next week.

> What *is the family doing ?* Moving.
>
> *Moving,* the present participle of the verb *to move,*
> is part of the compound verb tense.

IN GERMAN

Gerunds are usually expressed by a neuter noun made from the infinitive of the verb.

> lesen   →   **das** Lesen   *to read, reading*
>
> singen →   **das** Singen   *to sing, singing*

As you can see in the examples below, knowing how to distinguish a gerund from a present participle will enable you to select the correct form for German.

> **Talking** *is silver,* **being silent** *is gold.* ["Silence is golden."]
>
> > *What* is silver? Talking.
> >
> > *What* is gold? Being silent.
> >
> > *Talking* and *being silent* are gerunds.
>
> **Reden** ist Silber, **Schweigen** ist Gold.
>
> gerund verb   gerund verb

> *We* **are talking** *a lot.*
>
> > *What are we doing*? Talking.
> >
> > *Talking* is a present participle used in the present tense.
>
> Wir **reden** viel.
>
> verb

WHAT IS THE PAST PERFECT TENSE?

The PAST PERFECT TENSE, also called the PLUPERFECT, indicates that the action of the verb was completed in the past before another action or event in the past.

They *had* already *gone* by the time I arrived.

<pre>
      past perfect   simple past
          1   2
Both actions 1 and 2 occurred in the past, but action 1
preceded action 2. Therefore, action 1 is in the past perfect.
</pre>

IN ENGLISH

The past perfect is formed with the past tense auxiliary *had* + the past participle of the main verb: *I had walked, he had seen,* etc. (see p. 91 in *What is a Participle?*). In conversation, *had* is often shortened to *'d*.

Verb tenses indicate the time that an action occurs; therefore, when verbs in the same sentence are in the same tense, the actions took place at the same time. To show that actions took place at different times, different tenses must be used.

Look at the following examples.

The mother *was crying* because her son *was leaving*.

<pre>
     past progressive   past progressive
          1   1
     Action 1 and action 2 took place at the same time.
</pre>

The mother *was crying* because her son *had left*.

<pre>
     past progressive   past perfect
          1   2
        Action 2 took place before action 1.
</pre>

IN GERMAN

The past perfect, **das Plusquamperfekt**, is formed with the auxiliary verb **haben** *(to have)* or **sein** *(to be)* in the simple past tense + past participle of the main verb (see *What is the Past Tense?*, p. 87).

Wir **waren** schon ins Kino **gegangen**.

<pre>
simple past of sein (to be)   past participle of gehen (to go)
auxiliary in 2ⁿᵈ position   main verb at end of sentence
</pre>

*We **had** already **gone** to the movies.*

Wir **hatten** den Film schon **gesehen**.

<pre>
simple past of haben (to have)   past participle of sehen (to see)
auxiliary in 2ⁿᵈ position   main verb at end of sentence
</pre>

*We **had** already **seen** the film.*

Note the order of the verb parts: in the 2nd position, the conjugated past tense of the auxiliary and, at the end of the sentence, the past participle of the main verb.

Generally, the German past perfect is used the same way as the past perfect in English: to express an action or condition that ended before some other past action or condition that may or may not be stated. Notice how we can express the sequence of events by using different tenses.

VERB TENSE:		TIME ACTION TAKES PLACE
Present	0	now
Perfect or simple plast	-1	before 0
Past perfect	-2	before -1

Here is an example:

*They **had** already **left** when I **arrived**.*
Sie **waren** schon **abgefahren**, als ich **ankam**.
$\underbrace{\qquad\qquad}_{\text{past perfect -2}}$ $\underbrace{\qquad}_{\text{simple past -1}}$

CAREFUL — You cannot always rely on spoken English to determine when to use the past perfect in German. In conversation, if it is clear which action came first, English sometimes uses the simple past to describe an action that preceded another.

Anja *forgot* (that) she *saw* that movie.
$\underset{\text{simple past}}{|}$ $\underset{\text{simple past}}{|}$

Anja *forgot* (that) she *had seen* the movie.
$\underset{\text{simple past}}{|}$ $\underbrace{\qquad}_{\text{past perfect}}$

Although the two sentences above mean the same thing, only the sequence of tenses in the second sentence would be correct in German.

Gabi **hat vergessen**, dass sie den Film **gesehen hatte**.
$\underbrace{\qquad\qquad}_{\substack{\text{perfect} \\ \text{-1}}}$ $\underbrace{\qquad\qquad}_{\substack{\text{past perfect} \\ \text{-2}}}$

Both actions took place some time in the past. In German, the action of point -2 has to be in the past perfect because it took place before the action of point -1.

28

WHAT IS THE FUTURE PERFECT TENSE?

The **FUTURE PERFECT TENSE** indicates that the action of the verb will
occur in the future before another action or event in the future.

By the time we leave, he *will have finished.*

       future event   future perfect
           2   1

Both actions 1 and 2 will occur at some future time, but action 1 will be completed before action 2 takes place. Therefore, action 1 is in the future perfect tense.

I won't meet him. I *will have left* before he arrives.

       future perfect   future event
           1   2

Both action 1 and event 2 will occur at some future time, but action 1 will be completed before a specific event in the future. Therefore, action 1 is in the future perfect tense.

IN ENGLISH

The future perfect is formed with the auxiliary *will have* + the past participle of the main verb: *I will have walked, she will have gone* (see p. 91 in *What is a Participle?*). In conversation *will* is often shortened to *'ll.*

The future perfect is often used following expressions such as *by then, by that time, by* + a date.

    By the end of the month, he*'ll have graduated.*
    By June, I*'ll have saved* enough to buy a car.

IN GERMAN

The future perfect, **das Futur II,** is formed with the auxiliary verb **haben** *(to have)* or **sein** *(to be)* in the future tense + past participle of the main verb (see *What is the Future Tense?*, p. 85).

    Wir **werden** den Film **gesehen haben.**

              past paticiple of **sehen** *(to see)*
              + infinitive of auxiliary **haben**
              —— future tense of **haben** ——
    We **will have seen** the film.

Note the order of the verb parts: in the 2nd position, the conjugated future tense of the auxiliary and, grouped together at the end of the sentence, the past participle of the main verb followed by its auxiliary in the infinitive.

Generally, the German future perfect is used the same way as the future perfect in English: to express an action that will be completed in the future before some other future action or event, which may or may not be stated. Notice how we can express the sequence of events by using different tenses.

VERB TENSE:		TIME ACTION TAKES PLACE
Present	0	now
Future perfect	1	after 0 and before 2
Future	2	after 0 and after 1

Here is an example.

*They **will have left** before I arrive.*

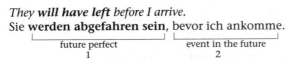

Sie **werden abgefahren sein**, bevor ich ankomme.

future perfect   event in the future
1   2

Both actions will take place some time in the future. In German, the action of point 1 has to be in the future perfect because it will take place before the event of point 2.

WHAT IS AN ADJECTIVE?

An ADJECTIVE is a word that describes a noun or a pronoun. There are different types of adjectives; they are classified according to the way they describe a noun or pronoun.

DESCRIPTIVE ADJECTIVE — A descriptive adjective indicates a quality; it tells what kind of noun it is (see p. 100).

> She read an *interesting* book.
> He has *brown* eyes.

POSSESSIVE ADJECTIVE — A possessive adjective shows possession; it tells whose noun it is (see p. 111).

> *His* book is lost.
> *Our* parents are away.

INTERROGATIVE ADJECTIVE — An interrogative adjective asks a question about a noun (see p. 116).

> *What* book is lost?
> *Which* book did you read?

DEMONSTRATIVE ADJECTIVE — A demonstrative adjective points out a noun (see p. 122).

> *This* teacher is excellent.
> *That* question is very appropriate.

IN ENGLISH

English adjectives usually do not change their form, regardless of the noun or pronouns described.

IN GERMAN

While English adjectives do not change their form, German adjectives change in order to agree with the case, gender, and number of the noun they modify. The various types of adjectives are discussed in separate sections.

CHAPTER

30

WHAT IS A DESCRIPTIVE ADJECTIVE?

1   A **DESCRIPTIVE ADJECTIVE**, also called a **QUALITATIVE ADJECTIVE**, is a word that indicates a quality of a noun or pronoun. As the name implies, it *describes* the noun or pronoun.

The book is *interesting.*
noun   descriptive
described   adjective

IN ENGLISH

A descriptive adjective does not change form, regardless of the noun or pronoun it modifies.

10   They are *intelligent.*
pronoun   adjective
described

She is an *intelligent* person.
pronoun   adjective
described

The form of the adjective *intelligent* remains the same although the persons described are different in number: *they* is plural and *person* is singular.

20   Descriptive adjectives are divided into two groups depending on how they are connected to the noun they modify.

Predicate adjectives — Predicate adjectives are connected to the noun they describe, always the subject of the sentence, by **LINKING VERBS** such as *to be, to feel, to look.* (See *What is a Predicate Noun?*, p. 43.)

The children are *good.*
noun   linking predicate
described   verb   adjective

30   The house looks *small.*
noun   linking predicate
described   verb   adjective

Attributive adjectives — Attributive adjectives are connected directly to the noun they describe and always precede it.

The *good* children were praised.
attributive   noun
adjective   described

The family lives in a *small* house.

               attributive   noun
               adjective   described

IN GERMAN

As in English, descriptive adjectives can be identified as predicate or attributive adjectives. While predicate adjectives do not take special endings, attributive adjectives do.

Predicate adjectives — Predicate adjectives have the same form as the dictionary entry for the adjective, regardless of the gender and number of the nouns or pronouns they modify.

*The chairs are **small**.*
Die Stühle sind **klein**.

    masculine plural

*The house is **small**.*
Das Haus ist **klein**.

    neuter singular

Attributive adjectives — Attributive adjectives change forms to agree with the noun they describe. They can have WEAK, STRONG, or MIXED ENDINGS depending on the case, gender, and number of the noun described usually indicated by the article preceding the noun (see p. 31 in *What is Meant by Case?*).

- weak ending if preceded by a **der**-word (such as a definite article)

  The **der**-word indicates the case, gender, and number of the noun; therefore, a weak ending suffices. The weak-endings are the most common adjective endings: **der** gelbe Fisch, **die** bunten Autos.

- strong ending if no article precedes the noun described

  A strong ending is added to the adjective itself to indicate its case, gender, and number: gelb**er** Fisch, blau**es** Auto.

- mixed endings if preceded by an **ein**-word (such as an indefinite article)

  Some cases use strong endings (nominative and accusative singular) → strong endings, other cases use weak endings: **ein** *gelber Fisch*, **einem** *gelben* Fisch. (Consult your textbook for details.)

Here are the steps to follow to choose the correct ending.

    1. Identify the adjective.

    2. Identify the noun described.

    3. Identify the case, gender, and number of noun above by looking at the word that precedes it

      • if definite article → adjective + weak ending

      • if no article → adjective + strong ending

      • if indefinite article → adjective + mixed ending

Here are some examples.

*Do you know the **new** student (female)?*
1. Adjective: new
2. Noun described: *the student* → **die** Studentin (feminine singular)
3. **die**: feminine singular accusative → weak ending → **-e**

Kennst du die **neue** Studentin?

*One can find it on the **first** page.*
1. Adjective: first
2. Noun described: *the page* → **die** Seite (feminine singular)
3. **der**: feminine singular dative (prep. **auf** + dative) → weak ending → **-en**

Man kann das auf der **ersten** Seite finden.

*I live in an **old** house.*
1. Adjective: old
2. Noun described: *a house* → **ein** Haus (neuter singular)
3. **einem**: neuter singular dative (prep. **in** + dative) → mixed ending → **-en**

Ich wohne in **einem** alten Haus.

*Gabi bought a **used** car.*
1. Adjective: used
2. Noun described: *a car* → **ein** Auto (neuter singular)
3. **ein**: neuter singular accusative → mixed ending → **-es**

Gabi hat ein **gebrauchtes** Auto gekauft.

*"**Blue** skies are on the way.*
1. Adjective: blue
2. Noun described: skies → Himmel (masculine singular)
3. No article: masculine singular nominative → strong ending → **-er**

Blauer Himmel kommt zum Vorschein.

Under the Study Tips below you will find charts of the various endings for attributive adjectives.

STUDY TIPS — DESCRIPTIVE ADJECTIVES

Pattern

Learning the patterns of adjective endings is more helpful than trying to learn the endings on their own. As you will see below, some of the forms will be similar to other forms you already know. Compare the pattern of the 3 types of endings of attributive adjectives.

DER-WORDS (weak endings)

	MASC.	**FEM.**	**NEUT.**	**PL.**
NOM.	der gelbe Fisch	die rote Blume	das blaue Auto	die bunten Autos
ACC.	den gelben Fisch	die rote Blume	das blaue Auto	die bunten Autos
DAT.	dem gelben Fisch	der roten Blume	dem blauen Auto	den bunten Autos
GEN.	des gelben Fisches	der roten Blume	des blauen Autos	der bunten Autos

What patterns do you see?
- endings → **-e** or **-en**
- nom. sing. endings → **-e**
- acc. sing. endings: fem. and neut. → **-e**; masc. → **-en**
- dative, genitive, and plural endings → **-en**

No ARTICLE (strong endings)

MASC.	FEM.	NEUT.	PL.
NOM. gelber Fisch	rote Blume	blaues Auto	bunte Autos
ACC. gelben Fisch	rote Blume	blaues Auto	bunte Autos
DAT. gelbem Fisch	roter Blume	blauem Auto	bunten Autos
GEN. gelbes Fisches	roter Blume	blaues Autos	bunter Autos

What pattern do you see?

■ endings → same as definite articles (see above and pp. 31-2).

EIN-WORDS (mixed endings)

MASC.	FEM.	NEUT.	PL.
NOM. ein gelber Fisch	eine rote Blume	ein blaues Auto	keine bunten Autos
ACC. einen gelben Fisch	eine rote Blume	ein blaues Auto	keine bunten Autos
DAT. einem gelben Fisch	einer roten Blume	einem blauen Auto	keinen bunten Autos
GEN. eines gelben Fisches	einer roten Blume	eines blauen Autos	keiner bunten Autos

What patterns do you see?

■ nom. and acc. sing. strong endings → same as definite articles
■ dat., gen., and pl. weak endings → –en

Practice

1. Create a list of common adjectives.
2. Write sentences using those adjectives as attributive adjectives with both **der**-words and **ein**-words to describe masc., fem., neut. sing. and pl. nouns functioning as subjects, indirect, and direct objects.

Subject → nominative case

> **Der junge Mann** geht ins Restaurant.
> *The young man goes to the restaurant.*

> **Ein junger Mann** geht ins Restaurant.
> *A young man goes to the restaurant.*

Direct object → accusative case

> Die Frau sieht **den jungen Mann**.
> *The woman sees **the young man**.*

> Die Frau sieht **einen jungen Mann**.
> *The woman sees **a young man**.*

Indirect object → dative case

> Die Frau gibt **dem jungen Mann** die Karte.
> *The woman gives **the young man** the menu.*

> Die Frau gibt **einem jungen Mann** die Karte.
> *The woman gives **a young man** the menu.*

Possessor → genitive case

> Der Hund **des jungen Mannes** sitzt neben ihm.
> *The young man's dog sits beside him.*

> Der Hund **eines jungen Mannes** sitzt neben ihm.
> *A young man's dog sits beside him*

130

140

150

160

CHAPTER

31

WHAT IS MEANT BY COMPARISON OF ADJECTIVES?

1 The term COMPARISON OF ADJECTIVES is used for descriptive adjectives which compare the degree of the same quality in two or more persons or things (see *What is a Descriptive Adjective?*, p. 100).

comparison of adjectives

Hansel is *tall* but Gretel is *taller*.

adjective   adjective
modifies *Hansel*   modifies *Gretel*

Both nouns, *Hansel* and *Gretel*, have the same quality indicated by the adjective *tall*, and we want to show that Gretel has a greater degree of that quality (i.e., she is *taller* than Hansel).

10 In English and in German, there are two types of comparison: comparative and superlative.

COMPARATIVE
The comparative compares a quality of a person or thing with the same quality in another person or thing. The comparison can indicate that one or the other has more, less, or the same amount of that quality.

IN ENGLISH
Let's go over the three degrees of comparison.

20 The comparative of GREATER DEGREE (more) is formed differently depending on the length of the adjective being compared.

- short adjective + *-er* + *than*

  Gretel is tall*er than* Hansel.
  Ingrid is young*er than* her sister.

- *more* + longer adjective + *than*

  Axel is *more* intelligent *than* Franz.
  His car is *more* expensive *than* ours.

The comparative of LESSER DEGREE (less) is formed as follows: *not as* + adjective + *as*, or *less* + adjective + *than*.

30 Hansel is *not as* tall *as* Gretel.
My car is *less* expensive *than* your car.

The comparative of EQUAL DEGREE (same) is formed as follows: as + adjective + as.

Axel is *as* tall *as* Franz.
My car is *as* expensive *as* his car.

IN GERMAN

As in English, the comparative has the same three degrees of comparison of adjectives. Unlike English, the structure used does not depend on the length of the adjective.

The comparative of GREATER DEGREE is formed by adding an umlaut to the stem vowels **a**, **o**, and **u** of the adjective + **-er**. The structure and the ending is different for predicate and attributive adjectives (see pp. 100-1).

- **predicate adjective** — The comparative is the two-word form: adjective + umlaut if necessary + **-er** + **als** *(than)*.

> Ingrid ist jünger **als** ihr Bruder.
>
> predicate adjective + umlaut + -er + als
> *Ingrid is younger **than** her brother.*

> Das Buch ist interessanter **als** der Film.
>
> predicate adjective + -er + als
> *The book is **more interesting than** the film.*

- **attributive adjective** — The comparative is the one-word form: adjective + umlaut if necessary + **-er-** + adjective ending, i.e., weak, strong, or mixed.

> Ich kenne das jüngere Mädchen nicht.
>
> attributive adjective + umlaut + -er- + weak ending
> *I don't know the younger girl.*

> Das ist ein interessanterer Film.
>
> attributive adjective + -er- + strong ending -er
> *That is a **more interesting** film.*

Do not confuse the comparative **–er** ending with the regular **–er** adjective ending.

REGULAR ADJECTIVE	COMPARATIVE ADJECTIVE
ein **bunter** Garten	ein bunter**er** Garten
*a **colorful** garden*	*a **more** colorful garden*
ein **kleiner** Hund	ein kleiner**er** Hund
*a **small** dog*	*a **smaller** dog*

As in English, the comparative of LESSER DEGREE does not require a change in the adjective. It is formed as follows: **nicht so** *(less)* + adjective + **wie** *(than)*.

> Tina ist **nicht so gross wie** Franz.
> *Tina is **not as tall as** Franz.*

> Tina ist **nicht so jung wie** Ingrid.
> *Tina is **not as young as** Ingrid.*

As in English, the comparative of EQUAL DEGREE does not require a change in the adjective. It is formed as follows: **so** *(as)* + adjective + **wie** *(as)*.

Axel ist **so gross wie** Anja.
*Axel is **as tall as** Anja.*

Mein Auto ist **so teuer wie** sein Auto.
*My car is **as expensive as** his car.*

SUPERLATIVE
The superlative form is used to stress the highest or lowest degrees of a quality.

IN ENGLISH
Let's go over the two degrees of the superlative.

The superlative of HIGHEST DEGREE is formed differently depending on the length of the adjective.

- *the* + short adjective + *-est*

  Ingrid is *the* calm*est* in the family.
  My car is *the* saf*est* on the market.

- *the most* + long adjective

  That argument was *the most* convincing.
  This book is *the most* interesting of all.

The superlative of LOWEST DEGREE is formed as follows: *the least* + adjective.

Hans is *the least* active.
Her car is *the least* expensive of all.

IN GERMAN
As in English, there are two degrees of the superlative.

The superlative of HIGHEST DEGREE is formed by adding an umlaut to the stem vowels **a**, **o**, and **u** + **-st** or **-est** to the stem of the adjective. The structure and the ending of the superlative form is different for predicate and attributive adjectives.

- **predicate adjective** — The superlative is the two word form: **am** + adjective + umlaut if necessary + (**-st-** or **-est-**) + **-en**.

  Dieses Buch ist **am ältesten**.
  *This book is **the oldest**.*

  Inge ist **am** klein**sten**.
  *Inge is **the smallest**.*

- **attributive adjective** — The superlative is the two-word form: definite article + adjective + umlaut if necessary + (**-st-** or **-est**) + weak adjective ending.

Hier ist **das älteste** Buch.
*Here is **the oldest** book.*

Inge ist **das kleinste** Mädchen in der Schule.
*Inge is **the smallest** girl in the school.*

The superlative of LOWEST DEGREE is a three-word form: **am wenigsten** + adjective.

Hans ist **am wenigsten** flexibel.
*Hans is **the least** flexible.*

Ihr Auto ist **am wenigsten** teuer.
*Her car is **the least** expensive.*

130

CAREFUL — In English and in German there are several adjectives that form the comparative and the superlative in irregular ways.

good	gut	*much*	viel
better	besser	*more*	mehr
best	am besten	*most*	am meisten

You will find a list of irregular comparative and superlative forms in your German textbook that you will have to memorize.

140

WHAT IS THE POSSESSIVE?

The **POSSESSIVE** is the form used to show that one noun *possesses* or owns another noun.

The teacher's German book is on her desk.
noun   noun
possessor   possessed

IN ENGLISH

There are two constructions to show possession.

Apostrophe — In this construction the possessor comes before the noun possessed.

- a singular possessor adds an apostrophe + "s"

  Gabi's mother

  the professor's book
  singular possessor

- a plural possessor ending with "s" adds an apostrophe after the "s"

  the girls' father

  the boys' school
  plural possessor

- a plural possessor not ending with "s" adds an apostrophe + "s"

  the children's playground

  the women's role
  plural possessor

The word "of" — In this construction the noun possessed comes before the possessor.

- a singular or plural possessor is preceded by *of the* or *of a*

  the book *of the* professor

  the branches *of a* tree
  singular possessor

  the teacher *of the* students
  plural possessor

- a proper noun possessor is preceded by *of*

  the poetry *of* Goethe
  proper noun possessor

IN GERMAN

There are also two ways to show possession: the genitive case is used in writing and in formal language and **von** + the dative case is used in spoken German (see *What is Meant by Case?*, p. 28).

Genitive case — When the genitive case of a noun is used to 40
show possession, the order in which the noun possessor and the noun possessed appear is different depending on whether the noun possessor is a proper or a common noun.

- proper noun possessor — This German structure parallels the English structure that uses the apostrophe to show possession. Just as in English, the noun possessor, in this case a proper noun, comes before the noun possessed.

> **Inges** Mutter
> *Inge's mother*
> | | 50
>   possessor possessed

In German the only time that an apostrophe is used for the genitive is when a proper noun ends in **-s** or **-z**.

> **Kiwus'** Gedichte
> *Kiwus's poems*
> | |
>   possessor possessed

- common noun possessor — This German structure parallels the English structure that uses *of*. Just as in English, the noun possessor, in this case a common noun, generally follows the noun possessed.   60

Most masculine and neuter singular nouns of one syllable → add **-es**. Masculine and neuter singular nouns of more than one syllable → add **-s**. The accompanying articles also end in **-s** (see pp. 31-2).

> der Sportler des Jahres
> | |
>   possessed   possessor
>   *athlete*   *year*
>   neuter singular
>   one syllable **Jahr**
>   genitive
>   definite article   70
>
> *the athlete **of the** year*
> *the year's (best) athlete*

Feminine singular and plural nouns → add **-er** to the preceding article or adjectives. The noun itself has no special ending.

der Mantel der Frau

possessed	possessor
coat	*woman*
	feminine

genitive
definite article

the coat of the woman
the woman's coat

Your German textbook will explain the genitive in greater detail and will point out the few irregularities.

Von + dative — When the construction **von** + dative case is used to show possession, the same construction is used for proper and common noun possessor. The order in which the noun possessor and the noun possessed appear corresponds to the construction *of* + noun possessor in English.

der Vater **von den** Mädchen

von + dative

the father of the girls

die Mutter **von** Inge
the mother of Inge

WHAT IS A POSSESSIVE ADJECTIVE?

A **POSSESSIVE ADJECTIVE** is a word that describes a noun by showing   1
who possesses that noun.

> Whose house is that? It's *my* house.
>> describes the noun *house*
>> and shows who possesses it, *I do*

IN ENGLISH

Like subject pronouns, possessive adjectives are identified
according to the person they represent (see p. 36).

SINGULAR POSSESSOR

1ST PERSON		my
2ND PERSON		your
3RD PERSON	MASCULINE	his
	FEMININE	her
	NEUTER	its

10

PLURAL POSSESSOR

1ST PERSON	our
2ND PERSON	your
3RD PERSON	their

A possessive adjective only identifies the possessor. The same
form is used regardless of the object possessed.   20

> Is that Axel's house? Yes, it is *his* house.
> Is that Ingrid's house? Yes, it is *her* house.
>> Although the object possessed is the same *(house)*, different possessive adjectives *(his* and *her)* are used because the possessors are different *(Axel* and *Ingrid)*.

> Is that Axel's house? Yes, it is *his* house.
> Are those Axel's keys? Yes, they are *his* keys.
>> Although the objects possessed are different *(house* and *keys)*, the same possessive adjective *(his)* is used because the possessor is the same *(Axel)*.

IN GERMAN   30

Like English, a German possessive adjective changes to identify
the possessor. Unlike English, however, and like all German
adjectives, it also agrees in case, gender, and number with the
noun possessed.

To choose the correct form of the possessive adjective follow
these steps:

1. Find the possessor.

SINGULAR POSSESSOR			
1ST **PERSON**		mein-	*my*
2ND **PERSON**	FAMILIAR	dein-	*your*
	FORMAL	Ihr-	*your*
	MASCULINE	sein-	*his*
3RD **PERSON**	FEMININE	ihr-	*her*
	NEUTER	sein-	*its*
PLURAL POSSESSOR			
1ST **PERSON**		unser-	*our*
2ND **PERSON**	FAMILIAR	euer-	*your*
	FORMAL	Ihr-	*your*
3RD **PERSON**		ihr-	*their*

2. Identify and analyze the noun possessed.
   - What is its case?
   - What is its gender?
   - What is its number?

3. Provide the ending that corresponds to the case, gender, and number of the noun possessed. These endings are the same as those for the indefinite articles (**ein, eine, ein**, see p. 24 and pp. 31-2). Because they follow the same pattern as indefinite articles, your textbook may refer to possessive adjectives as "**ein**-words."

Let us apply the above steps to examples.

> *He always forgets **his** books.*
>   1. POSSESSOR: *his* → **sein-**
>   2. NOUN POSSESSED: *books*
>   CASE: **vergessen** *(to forget)* takes a direct object → accusative
>   GENDER: **das Buch** *(book)* → neuter
>   NUMBER: *books* → plural
>   3. ENDING: accusative neuter plural → **-e**

Er vergißt immer **seine** Bücher.

> *She gives **her** brother the telephone number.*
>   1. POSSESSOR: *her* → **ihr-**
>   2. NOUN POSSESSED: *brother*
>   CASE: indirect object of **geben** *(to give)* → dative
>   (She gives the number *to whom?* Her brother.)
>   GENDER: **der Bruder** *(brother)* → masculine
>   NUMBER: *brother* → singular
>   3. ENDING: dative masculine singular → **-em**

Sie gibt **ihrem** Bruder die Telefonnummer.

CAREFUL — Remember that **ihr-** with an ending and followed by a noun is a possessive adjective that can mean *her* or *their* depending on possessor. If **ihr** has no ending and is not in front of a noun, it is a pronoun and it can mean either *you* (nominative, familiar plural) or *her* (dative singular).

80

STUDY TIPS — POSSESSIVE ADJECTIVES

Flashcard
Make a flashcard for each possessive pronoun. On the German side, write the possessive adjective with a dash following it to indicate that an ending it needed. On the English side, write the translation.

unser-	*our*
ihr-	*her, their*

Pattern
Review the case endings for indefinite articles pp. 31-2 in *What is Meant by Case?*. These are the endings for possessive adjectives.

90

WHAT IS A POSSESSIVE PRONOUN?

A **POSSESSIVE PRONOUN** is a word that replaces a noun and indicates the possessor of that noun. The word *possessive* comes from *possess,* to own.

> Whose house is that? It's *mine.*
>
> replaces the noun *house,* the object possessed,
> and shows who possesses it, *I do.*

IN ENGLISH

Like subject pronouns, possessive pronouns are identified according to the person they represent (see p. 36).

SINGULAR POSSESSOR

1ST **PERSON**		mine
2ND **PERSON**		yours
3RD **PERSON**	MASCULINE	his
	FEMININE	hers
	NEUTER	its

PLURAL POSSESSOR

1ST **PERSON**	ours
2ND **PERSON**	yours
3RD **PERSON**	theirs

A possessive pronoun only identifies the possessor. The same form is used regardless of the object possessed.

> My car is red; what color is Axel's? *His* is blue.
>
> 3rd pers. masc. sing.
>
> Axel's car is blue. What color is yours? *Mine* is white.
>
> 1st pers. sing.
>
> Although the object possessed is the same *(car),* different possessive pronouns
> *(his* and *mine)* are used because the possessors are different *(Axel* and *I).*

> Is that Axel's house? Yes, it is *his.*
>
> Are those Axel's keys? Yes, they are *his.*
>
> Although the objects possessed are different *(house* and *keys),* the same pos-
> sessive pronoun *(his)* is used because the possessor is the same *(Axel).*

IN GERMAN

Like English, a German possessive pronoun refers to the pos-sessor. Unlike English, however, and like all German pronouns, it also agrees in gender and number with the antecedent, that is, with the person or object possessed. In addition, the appropriate case ending is added to the possessive pronoun to reflect its function in the sentence.

Let us look at the German possessive pronouns to which the case endings are added.

SINGULAR POSSESSOR

1ST PERSON		mein-	*mine*
2ND PERSON	INFORMAL	dein-	*yours*
	FORMAL	Ihr-	*yours*
3RD PERSON	MASCULINE	sein-	*his*
	FEMININE	ihr-	*hers*
	NEUTER	sein-	*its*

PLURAL POSSESSOR

1ST PERSON		unser-	*ours*
2ND PERSON	INFORMAL	euer-	*yours*
	FORMAL	Ihr-	*yours*
3RD PERSON		ihr-	*theirs*

The case endings of possessive pronouns are essentially the same as those of the possessive adjectives (see p. 112 in *What is a Possessive Adjective?*). Possessive adjectives are more commonly used in German than the possessive pronoun. Your textbook will explain how to recognize possessive pronouns.

WHAT IS AN INTERROGATIVE ADJECTIVE?

An **INTERROGATIVE ADJECTIVE** is a word that asks for information about a noun.

> *Which* book do you want?
> asks information about the noun *book*

IN ENGLISH

The words *which* and *what* are called interrogative adjectives when they come in front of a noun and are used to ask a question about that noun.

> *Which* instructor is teaching the course?
> *What* courses are you taking?

IN GERMAN

The stem of the interrogative adjective is **welch-** *(which, what)*. Like all adjectives in German, the ending changes to agree in case, gender, and number with the noun modified. To choose the correct ending:

1. Identify and analyze the noun modified.
   - What is its case?
   - What is its gender and number?
2. Provide the ending that corresponds to the case, gender, and number of the noun modified. These endings are the same as those for the definite articles **der, die, das** (see p. 23). Because they follow the same pattern as definite articles, except in the neuter singular nominative and accusative where the ending **-es** replaces **-as**, your textbook may refer to interrogative adjectives as "**der**-words."

Let us apply the above steps to examples.

> *Which lamp is cheaper?*
>   1. NOUN MODIFIED: lamp
>   CASE: subject of *to be* **(sein)** → nominative
>   GENDER & NUMBER: **die Lampe** *(lamp)* → feminine singular
>   2. ENDING: nominative feminine singular → **-e**
> **Welche** Lampe ist billiger?

> *Which (what) dress do you want to wear?*
>   1. NOUN MODIFIED: dress
>   CASE: direct object of *to wear* **(tragen)** → accusative
>   GENDER & NUMBER: **das Kleid** *(dress)* → neuter singular
>   2. ENDING: accusative neuter singular → **-es**
> **Welches** Kleid willst du tragen?

***Which** man do we give our tickets to?*
1. NOUN MODIFIED: man
   CASE: indirect object of *to give* (**geben**) → dative
   GENDER & NUMBER: **der Mann** *(man)* → masculine singular
2. ENDING: dative masculine singular → **-em**
Welchem Mann geben wir unsere Karten?

INTERROGATIVE ADJECTIVE AS OBJECT OF A PREPOSITION
When expressing an English question with an interrogative adjective, be sure to restructure any dangling preposition (see pp. 66-7). Begin the question with the preposition, followed by the interrogative adjective in the case required by that preposition (see p.65).

***Which** street does he live **on**? → **On which** street does he live?*
1. NOUN MODIFIED: street
   CASE: object of preposition *on* (**in**) → dative
   GENDER & NUMBER: **die Straße** *(street)* → feminine singular
2. ENDING: dative feminine singular → **-er**
In welcher Straße wohnt er?

***What** film are you talking **about**? → **About what** film are you talking?*
1. NOUN MODIFIED: film
   CASE: object of preposition *about* (**über**) → accusative
   GENDER & NUMBER: **der Film** *(film)* → masculine singular
2. ENDING: accusative masculine singular → **-en**
Über welchen Film sprecht ihr?

CAREFUL — The word *what* is not always an interrogative adjective. It can also be an interrogative pronoun. When it is a pronoun, *what* is not followed by a noun. (See *What is an Interrogative Pronoun?*, p. 118).

What *is on the table?*
interrogative pronoun
Was ist auf dem Tisch?

It is important that you distinguish interrogative adjectives from interrogative pronouns because, in German, different words are used, and they follow different rules.

WHAT IS AN INTERROGATIVE PRONOUN?

An **INTERROGATIVE PRONOUN** is a word that replaces a noun and introduces a question. The word *interrogative* comes from *interrogate,* to question.

Who is coming for dinner?
question referring to a person

What did you eat for dinner?
question referring to a thing

In both English and German, a different interrogative pronoun is used depending on whether it refers to a "person" (human beings and live animals) or a "thing" (objects and ideas). In addition, the form of the interrogative pronoun often changes according to its function in the sentence: subject, direct object, indirect object, or object of a preposition. We shall look at each type separately.

REFERRING TO A PERSON
IN ENGLISH

There are three interrogative pronouns referring to persons.

Who is used for the subject of the sentence (see *What is a Subject?*, p. 40).

Who lives here?
subject

Who told you about that?
subject

Whom is used for the direct object, indirect object, and object of a preposition (see *What is an Object?*, p. 55 and pp. 64-5 in *What is a Preposition?*).

Whom do you know here?
direct object

(To) whom did you write a note?
indirect object

From whom did you get the book?
object of preposition *from*

In spoken English *who* is often used instead of *whom* for direct and indirect objects, and for objects of a preposition. It is only by asking the proper questions and restructuring dangling prepositions (see pp. 66-7) that you will be able to establish the function of the interrogative pronoun: is it a subject or an object of some kind?

> *Who* do you know here?
>> VERB: know
>> SUBJECT: Who knows? *You* → subject
>> OBJECT: You know who(m)? *Who* → object
> *Whom* do you know here?
>
> *Who* did you speak to?
>> DANGLING PREPOSITION: to
>> OBJECT: who → whom → object of preposition *to*
> *To whom* did you speak?

Whose, the possessive form, is used to ask about possession or ownership.

> There's a pencil on the floor? *Whose* is it?
>> possessive
>
> They are nice cars. *Whose* are they?
>> possessive

IN GERMAN

There are four forms of interrogative pronouns depending on the case required. Number and gender do not affect interrogative pronouns.

To select the proper form of the interrogative pronoun you will have to determine its function in the German sentence by asking the following five questions:

1. Is it the subject of the question?
2. Is it the direct object of the German verb? Does that verb take an accusative or dative direct object?
3. Is it the indirect object of the German verb?
4. Is it the object of a preposition? If so, does that German preposition take the accusative or dative?
5. Is it the possessive pronoun *whose*?

Subject — *who?* → (nom.) **wer?** — can refer to both singular and plural subjects.

> *Who is in the room? The teacher is in the room.*
> **Wer** ist in dem Zimmer? Die Lehrerin ist in dem Zimmer.
>
> *Who is coming this evening? Hans and Anja are coming.*
> **Wer** kommt heute abend? Hans und Anja kommen.

Object — *whom?* → (acc.) **wen?** or (dat.) **wem?** — depending on the case required in German. Be sure to restructure dangling prepositions (see pp. 66-7).

> *Who(m) do you see?*
> **Wen** sehen Sie?
>
> direct object → accusative

> *Who(m) are they helping?*
> **Wem** helfen sie?
>
> verb **helfen** *(to help)* → dative direct object

> *Who is he speaking **about?*** → ***About whom** is he speaking?*
> **Über wen** spricht er?
>
> preposition **über** *(about)* → accusative object

> *Who did he tell the story **to?*** → ***To whom** did he tell the story?*
> **Wem** hat er die Geschichte erzählt?
>
> indirect object → dative

> *Who are you coming **with?*** → ***With whom** are you coming?*
> **Mit wem** kommst du?
>
> preposition **mit** *(with)* → dative object

REFERRING TO A THING
IN ENGLISH

There is one interrogative pronoun referring to things or ideas. *What* is used for subject, direct object, indirect object, and the object of a preposition.

> *What* happened?
>
> subject

> *What* do you want?
>
> direct object

> *What* is the movie about?
>
> object of preposition *about*

CAREFUL — The word *what* is not always an interrogative pronoun. It can also be an interrogative adjective (see *What is an Interrogative Adjective?*, p. 116).

IN GERMAN

As in English, there is only one interrogative pronoun referring to things or ideas.

Was *(what)* is used as a subject or a direct object.

> **Was** ist in diesem Paket?
> *What is in this package?*

Was machst du?
What are you doing?

120

A construction called the **WO-COMPOUND** is used when the interrogative pronoun *what* is the object of some prepositions. It is formed by adding the prefix **wo-** (**wor-** if the preposition begins with a vowel) to the preposition.

Here are two examples.

What are you talking about?
Wovon redet ihr?

wo- + von *(about)*

130

What is he waiting for?
Worauf wartet er?

wor- + auf *(for)*

Your German textbook will discuss this construction and its use in greater detail.

SUMMARY

Here is a chart you can use as reference.

INTERROGATIVE PRONOUN		
REFERRING TO PERSONS		
NOMINATIVE	wer	*who*
ACCUSATIVE	wen	*whom*
DATIVE	wem	*whom*
GENITIVE	wessen	*whose*
REFERRING TO THINGS	was wo(r)- + prep.	*what*

140

STUDY TIPS — INTERROGATIVE PRONOUNS

Patterns

150

Compare the interrogative pronouns with the masculine forms of other parts of speech, such as personal pronouns and definite articles.

	Interrogative pronoun	Personal pronoun	Definite article
Nom.	wer	er	der
Acc.	wen	ihn	den
Dat.	wem	ihm	dem
Gen.	wessen		des

What similarities do you see?

-r, -n-, -m, -s mark the case of these pronouns and masculine articles.

- nominative forms end in **–r**
- accusative forms end in **–n**
- dative forms end in **–m**
- genitive forms have an **–s**

160

WHAT IS A DEMONSTRATIVE ADJECTIVE?

A **DEMONSTRATIVE ADJECTIVE** is a word used to refer to a specific noun.

This book is interesting.

refers to a specific *book* (noun)

IN ENGLISH

The demonstrative adjectives are *this* and *that* in the singular and *these* and *those* in the plural. They are rare examples of English adjectives agreeing in number with the noun they modify: *this* changes to *these* and *that* changes to *those* when they modify a plural noun (see *What is Meant by Number?*, p. 15).

SINGULAR	PLURAL
this cat	*these* cats
that man	*those* men

This and *these* refer to persons or objects near the speaker, and *that* and *those* refer to persons or objects away from the speaker.

IN GERMAN

The stems of the demonstrative adjectives are **dies-** *(this)*, **jen-** *(that)*, and **jed-** *(every)*. Like all adjectives in German, the ending changes to agree in case, gender, and number with the noun modified. To choose the correct ending:

1. Identify and analyze the noun modified.
   - What is its case?
   - What is its gender?
   - What is its number?
2. Provide the ending that corresponds to the case, gender, and number of the noun modified. These endings are the same as those for the definite articles (**der, die, das**, see p. 23 and pp. 31-2). Because they follow the same pattern as definite articles, except in the neuter singular nominative and accusative where the ending **-es** replaces **-as**, your textbook may refer to the demonstrative adjectives as "**der**-words."

Let us apply the above steps to some examples.

> **This** room is large.
>> 1. NOUN MODIFIED: room
>>> CASE: subject of **sein** *(to be)* → nominative
>>> GENDER & NUMBER: **das Zimmer** *(room)* → neuter singular
>> 2. ENDING: nominative neuter singular ending → **-es**
>
> **Dieses** Zimmer ist gross.

*Show **every** person the house.*

1. NOUN MODIFIED: person
   CASE: indirect object of **zeigen** *(to show)* → dative
   GENDER & NUMBER: **die Person** *(person)* → feminine singular
2. ENDING: dative feminine singular ending → **-er**

Zeig **jeder** Person das Haus.

*Have you seen **these** men?*

1. NOUN MODIFIED: men
   CASE: direct object of **sehen** *(to see)* → accusative
   GENDER: **der Mann** *(man)* → masculine plural
   NUMBER: **die Männer** *(men)* → plural
2. ENDING: accusative masculine plural ending → **-e**

Haben Sie **diese** Männer gesehen?

40

CHAPTER

38

WHAT IS A DEMONSTRATIVE PRONOUN?

A **DEMONSTRATIVE PRONOUN** is a word that stands for a noun as if pointing to it. The word *demonstrative* comes from *demonstrate*, to show. It refers to a previously expressed noun, called the **ANTECEDENT,** or to an entire statement.

Choose a book. *This one* is in English. *These* are in German.

antecedent   points to a book   points to other books

IN ENGLISH

The most common demonstrative pronouns are *this (one)* and *that (one)* to refer to one person or thing, and *these* and *those* to refer to more than one person or thing.

I have two groups of students. *These* speak German ; *those* do not.

antecedent   plural   plural
              close to speaker   further away

This (one), these refer to something or someone near the speaker, and *that (one), those* refer to things or persons further away from the speaker.

IN GERMAN

The most common demonstrative pronouns are the following:

dieser	*this, these*
jener	*that, those*

The demonstrative pronoun agrees in gender with its antecedent, its number depends on whether it refers to one thing *(this one, that one)* or to more than one person or object *(these, those)*, and its case depends on its function in the sentence.

To choose the correct form, follow these steps:
1. Determine the location of the item pointed out in relation to the speaker or the person spoken to.
2. Find the antecedent.
3. Determine the gender of the antecedent.
4. Determine the number of the antecedent: *this one, that one* → singular; *these, those* → plural.
5. Based on steps 2, 3, and 4 choose the German equivalent.
6. Add the case endings required by the function of the demonstrative pronoun.
7. Make a selection based on the steps 3-6 above.

Look at the following examples.

Which train should we take? Let's take **this one.**
  1. Relationship: this → near the speaker
  2. Antecedent: train (**Zug**)
  3. Gender: **der Zug** → masculine
  4. Number: *this one* → singular
  5. German word: **dies-**
  6. Case: direct object → accusative
  7. Selection: **dies-** + masc. sing, acc. → **-en**
Welchen Zug sollen wir nehmen? Nehmen wir **diesen.**

Do you know this woman? No, but I know **that one.**
  1. Relationship: that → further away from speaker
  2. Antecedent: woman (**Frau**)
  3. Gender: **die Frau** → feminine
  4. Number: *that one* → singular
  5. German word: **jen-**
  6. Case: direct object → accusative
  7. Selection: **jen-** + fem. sing. acc. → **-e**
Kennst du diese Frau? Nein, aber ich kenne **jene.**

CHAPTER

39

WHAT IS A SENTENCE?

A **SENTENCE** is a group of words that work together as a complete meaningful unit. In written form, a sentence begins with a capital letter and ends with a period, a question mark, or an exclamation point. Typically a sentence consists of at least a subject (see *What is a Subject?*, p. 40) and a verb (see *What is a Verb?*, p. 25).

> The girls ran.
> subject   verb

> They were eating.
> subject   verb

Depending on the verb, a sentence may also have direct and indirect objects (see *What is an Object?*, p. 55).

> The boy threw the ball.
> subject   verb   direct object

> Maria threw her brother the ball.
> subject   verb   indirect object   direct object

In addition, a sentence may include other words giving additional information about the subject or the verb; these words are called **MODIFIERS**. There are various kinds of modifiers:

- adjective (see *What is an Adjective?*, p. 99)

> I saw a *great* movie.
> adjective

- adverb (see *What is an Adverb?*, p. 140)

> *Yesterday* I saw a great movie.
> adverb

- prepositional phrase; that is, a group of words that begins with a preposition (see *What is a Preposition?*, p. 64)

> Yesterday *after work* I saw a great movie.
> prepositional phrase

- participial phrase; that is, a group of words that begins with a participle (see *What is a Participle?*, p. 90).

> *Attracted by the reviews*, I saw a great movie yesterday.
> participial phrase modifying *I*

- infinitive phrase; that is, a clause that begins with an infinitive (see *What is a Verb?*, p. 25).

> *To entertain* myself, I saw a movie.
> infinitive phrase

It is important for you to learn to recognize the different types of
sentences, clauses, modifiers, and phrases, since in German they
affect the order in which words appear in a sentence.

SIMPLE SENTENCES

A **SIMPLE SENTENCE** is a sentence consisting of only one **CLAUSE,**
namely, a group of words including a subject and a conjugated
verb.

IN ENGLISH

There is no set position for the verb in an English sentence or
clause, but the subject almost always comes before the verb.

> We are going to the concert.
> subject verb

A modifier can also come before the subject.

> *Today* we are going to a concert.
> adverb

> *After the party* we are going to a concert.
> prepositional phrase

IN GERMAN

In a simple sentence the conjugated verb always stands in
second position. This does not mean that the verb is always
the second word in the sentence, because some groups of
words, such as prepositional phrases, count as one position.

> Wir **essen** in einem Restaurant.
> *we **are eating** in a restaurant*
> subject verb
> 1 2

> Heute **essen** wir in einem Restaurant.
> *today **are eating** we in a restaurant*
> adverb verb subject
> 1 2
> *Today we **are eating** in a restaurant.*

> Vor der Party **essen** wir in einem Restaurant.
> *before the party **are going** we to a concert*
> prep. phrase verb subject
> 1 2
> *Before the party we **are eating** in a restaurant.*

As you can see, only in the first example is it possible to put
the subject before the verb. In the other two sentences where
there is a modifier in the first position, the subject must follow
the verb so that the verb can be in the second position.

COMPOUND SENTENCES

A COMPOUND SENTENCE consists of two main clauses, each with a subject and a conjugated verb, joined by a coordinating conjunction (see *What is a Conjunction?*, p. 136). In each clause, the word order is the same as in a simple sentence.

IN ENGLISH

As in a simple sentence, the position of the verb in each clause may vary, though the subject usually comes before the verb. In the examples below, each clause is underlined.

The sky is grey, *but* it is not raining.
　　　　　　　｜
　　　　coordinating conjunction

Every evening John plays the piano *and* his sister sings.
　　　　　　　　　　　　　　　　　　｜
　　　　　　　　　　　coordinating conjunction

IN GERMAN

It is important that you know how to recognize a compound sentence because the verb must be in the second position of each clause. The coordinating conjunction is just a link between the two simple sentences and does not count as the first position.

Der Himmel **ist** grau, aber es **regnet** nicht.
　　　｜　　　｜　　　　｜　　｜　　　｜
　　　1　　　2　　　conj.　1　　2
the　　sky　　is　grey,　but　　it　is raining not
*The sky **is** grey, but it **is** not **raining**.*

Jeden Abend **spielt** Max Klavier und seine Schwester **singt**.
└────────┘　　｜　　　　　　　　　｜　└──────────┘　　｜
　　1　　　　　2　　　　　　　conj.　　　1　　　　　　2
every evening　　plays　Max　the piano　and　　his sister　　　　sings
*Every evening Max **plays** the piano and his sister **sings**.*

COMPLEX SENTENCES

A COMPLEX SENTENCE is a sentence consisting of a main clause and one or more dependent clauses. In the examples below the main clause is underlined; the remainder of the sentence is the dependent clause.

The MAIN CLAUSE, also called an INDEPENDENT CLAUSE, is a clause that could stand alone as a complete sentence.

The DEPENDENT CLAUSE, also called a SUBORDINATE CLAUSE, cannot stand alone as a complete sentence because it depends on the main clause for its full meaning.

Before I eat, I always wash my hands.

It makes sense to say "I always wash my hands" without the first clause in the sentence; therefore, it is the main clause. It does not make sense to say, "before I eat" unless we add a conclusion; therefore, it is the dependent clause.

IN ENGLISH

Distinguishing a main clause from a dependent clause helps you to write complete sentences and to avoid sentence fragments.

IN GERMAN

It is important for you to learn to distinguish between a main clause and a dependent clause in German, because each type of clause has its own word order rules.

MAIN CLAUSE — the word order depends on whether the main clause is at the beginning of the sentence or at the end.

■ at the beginning of the sentence — the verb of the main clause remains in the same position as in the simple sentence; that is, in the second position.

> Ich **wasche** mir immer die Hände, bevor ich esse.
> | |
> 1   2
> *I   wash   myself always the hands   before   I   eat*
> *I always **wash** my hands before I eat.*

■ at the end of the sentence — the verb of the main clause comes right after the dependent clause that functions as a single unit of meaning and counts as the first position.

> Bevor ich esse, **wasche** ich mir immer die Hände.
> |_____| |
>   1   2
> *before   I   eat,   wash   I   myself   always   the hands*
> *Before I eat, I always **wash** my hands.*

DEPENDENT CLAUSES — the conjugated verb always stands at the end of the dependent clause, regardless if it comes before or after the main clause.

> Ich wasche mir die Hände, weil sie schmutzig **sind**.
> *I   wash   myself the hands   because they   dirty   are*
> *I wash my hands, because they **are** dirty.*

> Weil sie schmutzig **sind**, wasche ich mir die Hände.
> *because they dirty   are   wash   I   myself the hands*
> *Because they **are** dirty, I wash my hands.*

Your German textbook will explain this structure in more detail.

130

140

150

CHAPTER
40

WHAT ARE AFFIRMATIVE AND
NEGATIVE SENTENCES?

¹ A sentence can be classified according to whether or not the verb is negated, that is, made negative with the word *not*.

An **AFFIRMATIVE SENTENCE** is a sentence whose verb is not negated. It states a fact that is, i.e., a positive fact.

> Austria is a country in Europe.
> Jade will work at the university.
> They liked to travel.

A **NEGATIVE SENTENCE** is a sentence whose verb is negated with the word *not*. It states a fact that is not, i.e., a negative fact.

¹⁰
> Austria is *not* a country in Asia.
> Jade will *not* work at the university.
> They *did not* like to travel.

IN ENGLISH

An affirmative sentence can be made negative in one of two ways:

- by adding *not* after auxiliary verbs or modals (see *What is an Auxiliary Verb?*, p. 76)

AFFIRMATIVE	NEGATIVE
Axel *is* a student.	Axel is *not* a student.
Jade *can* do it.	Jade can*not* do it.
They *will* travel.	They will *not* travel.

²⁰

The word *not* is often attached to the auxiliary and the letter "o" replaced by an apostrophe; this is called a **CONTRACTION**: is not → isn't; cannot → can't; will not → won't.

- by adding the auxiliary verb *do, does,* or *did + not* followed by the dictionary form of the main verb

AFFIRMATIVE	NEGATIVE
We *study* a lot.	We *do not* study a lot.
Max *writes* well.	Max *does not* write well.
The train *arrived*.	The train *did not* arrive.

³⁰

The words *do, does, did* are often contracted with *not:* do not → don't; does not → doesn't; did not → didn't.

IN GERMAN

Unlike English, which always uses *not* to make an affirmative sentence negative, German uses either **nicht** or **kein** depending on the part of speech being negated.

- to negate verbs and other parts of speech → **nicht** *(not)*

  Nicht never changes form, but its position in the sentence varies: **nicht** follows all personal pronouns, the subject, verb, direct object, and expressions of definite time, and precedes everything else in the sentence. Let's look at some examples.

AFFIRMATIVE	**NEGATIVE**
Ich sehe dich.	Ich sehe dich **nicht**.
	personal pronoun + **nicht**
I see you.	*I **don't** see you.*
Er arbeitet in Berlin.	Er arbeitet **nicht** in Berlin.
	verb + **nicht** + prepositional phrase
He works in Berlin.	*He **doesn't** work in Berlin.*
Sie besucht Anna oft.	Sie besucht Anna **nicht** oft.
	direct object + **nicht** + adverb
She visits Anna often.	*She **doesn't** visit Anna often.*
Er kommt morgen abend.	Er kommt morgen abend **nicht**.
	definite time + **nicht**
He is coming tomorrow night.	*He is **not** coming tomorrow night.*

  Your textbook will discuss the position of **nicht** in greater detail.

- to negate a non-specific noun; i.e., a noun preceded by an indefinite article or no article → **kein** *(not a, not any, no)*

  Kein agrees in case, gender, and number with the noun it precedes and takes the same endings as **ein**-words (see pp. 31-2).

AFFIRMATIVE	**NEGATIVE**
Anna sieht **einen** Hund.	Anna sieht **keinen Hund**.
indefinite article	masc. sing. acc. (direct object)
*Anna sees **a** dog.*	*Anna sees **no dog**.*
	[Anna doesn't see a dog.]
Ich habe Zeit.	Ich habe **keine Zeit**.
no article	fem. sing. acc. (direct object)
I have time.	*I have **no time**.*
	[I don't have time.]
Studenten wohnen hier.	**Keine Studenten** wohnen hier.
no article	masc. pl. nom. (subject)
Students live here.	***No students** live here.*

CAREFUL — Remember that in negative sentences in German there is no equivalent for the auxiliary words *do, does, did*; do not try to include them.

NEGATIVE WORDS

In both English and German there are other negative words besides *not* that can be added to an affirmative sentence.

IN ENGLISH

The most common negative words are *nothing, nobody, no one,* which can be used as subjects or objects of a sentence.

> *Nothing* is free.
> *Nobody* is going to the movies.
> subject

> I see *nothing*.
> I see *no one (nobody)*.
> object

IN GERMAN

The most common negative words are **nichts** *(nothing)* and **niemand** *(no one, nobody)*. As in English they can be used as subjects or objects of a sentence.

■ subject of the sentence

> **Nichts** ist umsonst.
> *Nothing is free.*

> **Niemand** geht ins Kino.
> *No one is going to the movies.*

■ object of the sentence — **nichts** doesn't change regardless of its function; **niemand** can be either in the masculine accusative (**-en**) or the masculine dative (**-em**) depending on the verb.

> Ich sehe **nichts**.
> *I see **nothing**.*

> Ich sehe **niemanden**.
> sehen *(to see)* takes an accusative object
> *I see **no one**.*

> Er hilft **niemandem**.
> helfen *(to help)* takes dative object
> *He helps **no one**.*

CAREFUL — Note the spelling difference between **nicht** *(not)* and **nichts** *(nothing)*.

WHAT ARE DECLARATIVE AND INTERROGATIVE SENTENCES?

A sentence can be classified as to whether it is making a statement 1
or asking a question.

A **DECLARATIVE SENTENCE** is a sentence that makes a statement.

> Franz arrived in Frankfurt at 11:15 A.M.

An **INTERROGATIVE SENTENCE** is a sentence that asks a question.

> Did Franz arrive in Frankfurt at 11:15 A.M?
> When did Franz arrive in Frankfurt?

In written language, an interrogative sentence always ends with a
question mark.

IN ENGLISH   10

There are two types of interrogative sentences: questions that
can be answered by "yes" or "no" and questions that ask for
information.

Yes-or-no questions — Questions are formed from a declarative
sentence in one of two ways:

- by adding the auxiliary verb *do, does,* or *did* before the subject
  + the dictionary form of the main verb.

DECLARATIVE SENTENCE	INTERROGATIVE SENTENCE
Ingrid *likes* the class.	*Does* Ingrid *like* the class?
Axel and Julia *sing* well.	*Do* Axel and Julia *sing* well?
Franz *went* to Berlin.	*Did* Franz *go* to Berlin?

20

- by inverting the normal word order of subject + verb to verb +
  subject. This **INVERSION** can only be used with auxiliary verbs or
  auxiliary words (see *What is an Auxiliary Verb?*, p. 76).

DECLARATIVE SENTENCE	INTERROGATIVE SENTENCE
Franz is home.	*Is* Franz home?
subject + verb *to be*	verb + subject
You have received a letter.	*Have you received* a letter?
subject + *have* + main verb	*have* + subject + main verb

30

She will come tomorrow.	*Will she come* tomorrow?
subject + *will* + main verb	*will* + subject + main verb

Asking for information — Questions start with a question word,
such as *when, who, which,* and *how,* + the interrogative sentence
as formed above.

interrogative sentence

Why does Julia like the class?
Where did Ingrid go?

IN GERMAN

As in English, there are two types of interrogative sentences: yes-or-no questions and question word questions.

Yes-or-no questions — Questions are formed by the inversion process, i.e., by moving the conjugated verb from its second position in a declarative sentence to the first position and following it with the subject.

DECLARATIVE SENTENCE	INTERROGATIVE SENTENCE
Julia hat den Kurs gern.	**Hat Julia** den Kurs gern?
1 subject + 2 conjugated verb	1 conjugated verb + 2 subject
Julia likes the class.	*Does Julia like the class?*
Morgen **kommt sie** wieder.	**Kommt sie** morgen wieder?
1 verb + 2 subject	1 verb + 2 subject
She is coming again tomorrow.	*Is she coming again tomorrow?*

Asking for information — Questions start with a question word, such as **wann** *(when)*, **wo** *(where)*, **warum** *(why)*, **wie oft** *(how often)*, + the interrogative sentence as formed above.

interrogative sentence

Warum hat Julia den Kurs gern?
Why does Julia like the class?

interrogative sentence

Wann kommt sie wieder?
When is she coming again?

CAREFUL — Remember that in interrogative sentences there is no equivalent for the auxiliary words *do, does, did* in German; do not try to include them.

TAG QUESTIONS

In both English and German when you expect a yes-or-no answer, you can also transform a statement into a question by adding a short phrase called a TAG at the end of the statement.

IN ENGLISH

The tense of the statement dictates the tense of the tag and affirmative statements take negative tags and negative statements take affirmative tags (see *What are Affirmative and Negative Sentences?*, p. 130).

affirmative statement   negative tag

Axel and Ingrid *are* friends, *aren't they?*   80

      present   present

Axel and Ingrid *were* friends, *weren't they?*

      past   past

negative statement   affirmative tag

Axel and Ingrid *aren't* friends, *are they?*

      present   present

Axel and Ingrid *weren't* friends, *were they?*

      past   past   90

IN GERMAN

When confirmation is expected, the words **nicht wahr** or **oder** can be added to a statement. **Oder** can be used with either positive or negative statements, but **nicht wahr** is used only with affirmative statements.

Du kommst heute nicht mit, **oder?**
*You aren't coming along today, **are you?***

affirmative statement

Sie wohnt in Berlin, **nicht wahr?**
*She lives in Berlin, **doesn't she?***   100

WHAT IS A CONJUNCTION?

A **CONJUNCTION** is a word that links two or more words or groups of words.

> He had to choose between good *and* evil.
> |
> conjunction

> They left *because* they were bored.
> |
> conjunction

> Let me know *when* you will arrive.
> |
> conjunction

IN ENGLISH

There are two kinds of conjunctions: coordinating and subordinating.

A **COORDINATING CONJUNCTION** joins words, phrases (groups of words without a verb), and clauses (groups of words with a verb) that are equal; it *coordinates* elements of equal rank. The major coordinating conjunctions are *and, but, or, nor, for,* and *yet.*

> good *or* evil
> word   word

> over the river *and* through the woods
> phrase   phrase

> They invited us *but* we couldn't go.
> clause   clause

In the last example, each of the two clauses, "they invited us" and "we couldn't go," expresses a complete thought; each clause is, therefore, a complete sentence that could stand alone. When a clause expresses a complete sentence it is called a **MAIN CLAUSE**. In the above sentence, the coordinating conjunction *but* links two main clauses (see p. 128 in *What is a Sentence?*).

A **SUBORDINATING CONJUNCTION** joins a main clause to a dependent clause; it *subordinates* one clause to another. A **DEPENDENT CLAUSE** does not express a complete thought; it is, therefore, not a complete sentence. A clause introduced by a subordinating conjunction is called a **SUBORDINATE CLAUSE**. Typical subordinating conjunctions are *before, after, since, although, because, if, unless, so that, while, that,* and *when.*

In the following examples, the subordinate clauses are underlined, the remaining words correspond to the main clause.

Although we were invited, we didn't go.

|
subordinating
conjunction

They left *because* they were bored.

|
subordinating
conjunction

He said *that* he was tired.

|
subordinating
conjunction

Notice that the subordinate clauses don't express a complete thought and may come either at the beginning of the sentence or after the main clause.

IN GERMAN

As in English, German has coordinating and subordinating conjunctions. Like adverbs and prepositions, conjunctions never change their form.

The major coordinating conjunctions are **und** *(and)*, **oder** *(or)*, **aber** *(but)*, and **denn** *(for)*. Typical subordinating conjunctions include **als** *(when)*, **weil** *(because)*, **wenn** *(if, whenever)*, **dass** *(that)*, **bevor** *(before)*, **während** *(while),* and **nachdem** *(after)*.

As in English, the subordinate clause may come before or after the main clause. Unlike English where the word order remains the same regardless of the type of clause, German subordinating conjunctions affect word order in the subordinate clause and the main clause.

- in the subordinate clause the conjugated verb is always placed at the end of the clause
  Ich fahre mit dem Bus, **weil** ich kein Auto **habe**.

      | |
  subordinating   verb at the end
  conjunction   of the subordinate clause
  *I go by bus **because** I have no car.*

- if the subordinate clause comes at the beginning of the sentence, it functions as the first element in the sentence and the conjugated verb of the main clause is placed in the 2ⁿᵈ position, right after the conjugated verb of the subordinate clause, separated by a comma.

      1ˢᵗ position   2ⁿᵈ position
  subordinate clause |
  Weil ich kein Auto **habe**, **fahre** ich mit dem Bus.

              | |
      conjugated verb   conjugated verb of main clause
  Because I have no car, I go by bus.

PREPOSITION OR CONJUNCTION?
IN ENGLISH

Some words function as both prepositions and subordinating conjunctions, for example, *before* and *after*. We can identify the word's function by determining whether or not it introduces a clause.

- if the word in question introduces a clause, i.e., a group of words with a verb, it is a subordinating conjunction.

  We left *before* the intermission began.
  sub. conj. subject + verb → clause

  After the concert was over, we ate ice cream.
  sub. conj. subject + verb → clause

- if the word in question is followed by an object, but no verb, it is a preposition.

  We left *before* the intermission.
  prep.   object of preposition

  After the concert we ate ice cream.
  prep.   object of preposition

IN GERMAN

It is important for you to establish whether a word is a preposition or a conjunction because in German you will use different words and apply different rules of grammar depending on the part of speech.

English PREPOSITION AND CONJUNCTION	GERMAN	
	PREPOSITION	CONJUNCTION
before	vor	bevor
after	nach	nachdem

Let us look at some examples using these different parts of speech.

- *before* and *after* as conjunctions → **bevor** and **nachdem** connect two clauses and require two parts of speech, i.e., a subject and a verb.

  *We left **before** the intermission began.*
  subject + verb
  Wir sind weggegangen, **bevor** die Pause anfing.

  After the concert was over, we ate ice cream.
  subject + verb
  Nachdem das Konzert vorbei war, aßen wir Eis.

- *before* and *after* as prepositions → **vor** and **nach** are part of a phrase and require one part of speech, i.e., an object.

    *We left **before** the intermission.*

    object
    Wir sind **vor** der Pause weggegangen.

    ***After** the concert we ate ice cream.*

    object   130
    Nach dem Konzert haben wir Eis gegessen.

CAREFUL — In order to choose the correct German word and apply the appropriate rules of grammar, be sure to distinguish between a conjunction and a preposition: a conjunction introduces a clause and requires a subject and a verb, while a preposition requires only an object.

STUDY TIPS — CONJUNCTIONS

Flashcard
                                                                         140
1. Make a flashcard for each conjunction. On the English side, write the meaning of the conjunction. On the German side, write "coordinating" or "subordinating" and a sample sentence from your textbook.
2. Sort the flashcards into two categories: coordinating and subordinating. To remember the five cards in the coordinating pile: **sondern, oder, denn, aber, und**, use the acronym **SODAund.** All the other conjunctions belong in the subordinating category.

CHAPTER

43

WHAT IS AN ADVERB?

An **ADVERB** is a word that describes a verb, an adjective, or another adverb. It indicates manner, degree, time, place.

Julia drives *well*.
verb adverb

The house is *very* big.
adverb adjective

The girl ran *too quickly*.
adverb adverb

In English and in German, the structure for comparing adverbs is the same as the structure for comparing predicate adjectives (see *What is Meant by Comparison of Adjectives?*, p. 104).

IN ENGLISH

There are different types of adverbs.

- an **ADVERB OF MANNER** answers the question *how?*

  Ingrid sings *beautifully*.

  Adverbs of manner are the most common and they are easy to recognize because they end with *-ly*.

- an **ADVERB OF DEGREE** answers the question *how much?*

  Axel did *well* on the exam.

- an **ADVERB OF TIME** answers the question *when?*

  He will come *soon*.

- an **ADVERB OF PLACE** answers the question *where?*

  The children were left *behind*.

A few adverbs in English are identical in form to the corresponding adjectives (see *What is an Adjective?*, p. 99).

ADVERB	**ADJECTIVE**
The guests came *late*.	We greeted the *late* guests.
Don't drive so *fast*.	*Fast* drivers cause accidents.
She works very *hard*.	This is *hard* work.

CAREFUL — Remember that in English *good* is an adjective since it modifies a noun and *well* is an adverb since it modifies a verb.

The student writes *good* English.
    Good modifies the noun *English;* it is an adjective.

The student writes *well*.
    Well modifies the verb *writes;* it is an adverb.

IN GERMAN

As in English, there are words that function only as adverbs.

Das Haus ist **sehr** groß.
*The house is **very** big.*

Er kommt **bald**.
*He is coming **soon**.*

In German however, many adverbs, particularly adverbs of manner, have the same form as their corresponding adjective.

ADVERB	ADJECTIVE
Du hast das **gut** gemacht.	Dieses Buch ist **gut**.
*You did that **well**.*	*This book is **good**.*
Sie singen **schön**.	Das Lied ist **schön**.
*They sing **beautifully**.*	*The song is **beautiful**.*
Wir fahren **schnell**.	Der Wagen ist **schnell**.
*We drive **fast**.*	*The car is **fast**.*

The most important fact for you to remember is that adverbs are invariable; i.e., unlike German adjectives they never change form.

CAREFUL — In English, the word order for adverbs is manner + place + time. In German, it is time + manner + place.

*I am traveling by train to Munich **tomorrow**.*
    manner place   time

Ich fahre **morgen** mit dem Zug nach München.
  time   manner   place

Consult your textbook for the placement of adverbs.

STUDY TIPS — ADVERBS

Flashcards

Create flashcards for each German adverb you learn and its English equivalent. Note when it may be used as an adverb and adjective or as an adverb only.

früh	*early*	adjective & adverb
nie	*never*	adverb
langsam	*slow, slowly*	adjective, adverb

CHAPTER

44

WHAT IS A RELATIVE PRONOUN?

A **RELATIVE PRONOUN** is a word used at the beginning of a clause that gives additional information about someone or something previously mentioned.

clause
additional information about *the book*

I'm reading the book *that* the teacher recommended.

A relative pronoun serves two purposes:

- as a pronoun it stands for a noun previously mentioned. The noun to which it refers is called the **ANTECEDENT**.

Here comes the boy *who* broke the window.

antecedent of the relative pronoun *who*

- it introduces a **SUBORDINATE CLAUSE,** also called a **DEPENDENT CLAUSE**; that is, a group of words having a subject and a verb that cannot stand alone because it does not express a complete thought. A subordinate clause is dependent on a **MAIN CLAUSE**; that is, another group of words having a subject and a verb that can stand alone as a complete sentence (see p. 127 in *What is a Sentence?*).

main clause   subordinate clause

Here comes the boy *who broke the window.*

verb   subject   subject   verb

A subordinate clause that starts with a relative pronoun is also called a **RELATIVE CLAUSE**. In the example above, the relative clause starts with the relative pronoun *who* and gives us additional information about the antecedent *boy*.

Relative clauses are very common. We use them in everyday speech without giving much thought as to how we construct them. The relative pronoun allows us to combine two thoughts, which have a common element, into a single sentence. In this chapter, the relative clauses are underlined.

COMBINING SENTENCES WITH A RELATIVE PRONOUN

When sentences are combined with a relative pronoun, the relative pronoun can have different functions in the relative clause. It can be the subject, the direct object, the indirect object, or the object of a preposition.

Let us look at some examples of how sentences are combined.

- relative pronoun as a subject (see p. 40)

  SENTENCE A The students passed the exam.
  SENTENCE B They studied.

  1. COMMON ELEMENT — Identify the element sentences A and B have in common.

     Both *the students* and *they* refer to the same persons.

  2. ANTECEDENT — The common element in sentence A will be the antecedent of the relative pronoun. The common element in sentence B will be replaced by a relative pronoun.

     The students is the antecedent. *They* will be replaced by a relative pronoun.

  3. FUNCTION — The relative pronoun in the relative clause has the same function as the word it replaces.

     They is the subject of *studied*. It will be replaced by a subject relative pronoun.

  4. PERSON OR THING — Identify whether the antecedent refers to a person(s) or a thing(s).

     The antecedent *students* refers to persons.

  5. SELECTION — Choose the relative pronoun according to its function (step 3) and its antecedent (step 4).

     who (or *that* see p. 144, l. 108-10)

  6. RELATIVE CLAUSE — Place the relative pronoun at the beginning of sentence B, thus forming a relative clause.

     who (that) studied

  7. PLACEMENT — To combine the two clauses, place the relative clause right after its antecedent.

     The students *who (that) studied* passed the exam.

- relative pronoun as a direct object (see p. 55)

  SENTENCE A This is the student.
  SENTENCE B I saw him.

     1. COMMON ELEMENT: *the student* and *him*
     2. ANTECEDENT: the student
     3. FUNCTION: *him* is the direct object
     4. PERSON OR THING: *the student* is a person
     5. SELECTION: *that* or *whom*
     6. RELATIVE CLAUSE: *that (whom)* I saw
     7. PLACEMENT: the student + *that (whom)* I saw

  This is the student *(that, whom)* I saw.

■ relative pronoun as an indirect object (see p. 57)

(see p. 57)

80

SENTENCE A   This is the student.
SENTENCE B   I spoke to him.

1. COMMON ELEMENT: *the student* and *him*
2. ANTECEDENT: the student
3. FUNCTION: *him* is the indirect object
4. PERSON OR THING: *the student* is a person
5. SELECTION: *to whom*
6. RELATIVE CLAUSE: *to whom* I spoke
7. PLACEMENT: the student + *to whom* I spoke

This is the student *to whom* I spoke.

90

■ relative pronoun as an object of a preposition (see pp. 64-5)

(see pp. 64-5)

SENTENCE A   This is the student.
SENTENCE B   I spoke with him.

1. COMMON ELEMENT: *the student* and *him*
2. ANTECEDENT: the student
3. FUNCTION: *him* is the object of the preposition *with*
4. PERSON OR THING: *the student* is a person
5. SELECTION: *whom*
6. RELATIVE CLAUSE: *with whom* I spoke
7. PLACEMENT: the student + *with whom* I spoke

This is the student *with whom* I spoke.

100

SELECTION OF A RELATIVE PRONOUN
IN ENGLISH

The selection of a relative pronoun in English depends not only on its function in the relative clause, but also on whether its antecedent is a "person" (human beings and animals) or a "thing" (objects and ideas). In standard and written English, *who* or *whom* are the relative pronouns used to refer to persons. In spoken English, they are often replaced by *that*. Moreover, in certain functions the relative pronoun is omitted altogether.

110

STANDARD: The teacher *(whom)* you wanted to see is not here.
SPOKEN: The teacher *(that)* you wanted to see is not here.

The distinction between spoken and standard English is important. In this chapter make sure you refer to standard English, which includes a relative pronoun.

IN GERMAN

Unlike English, the same set of relative pronouns is used for antecedents referring to persons and things and, more importantly, relative pronouns can never be omitted.

German relative pronouns are based on two factors:

120

1. GENDER AND NUMBER — the gender and number of the antecedent.
2. CASE FORM — their function in the relative clause

We shall look at each function separately. Notice that relative clauses are always separated by a comma from the main clause.

SUBJECT OF THE RELATIVE CLAUSE
(see *What is a Subject?*, p. 40)

IN ENGLISH

There are three relative pronouns that can be used as subjects of a relative clause, depending on whether the relative pronoun refers to a person or a thing. When it is the subject of a relative clause, the relative pronoun is never omitted. — 130

Person — *who* (or *that*) → subject of the relative clause

> She is the only student <u>*who (that)* answered all the time.</u>

Thing — *which* or *that* → subject of the relative clause

> The movie <u>*which* is so popular</u> was filmed in Germany.
> The movie <u>*that* is so popular</u> was filmed in Germany.

Notice that the relative pronoun subject is always followed by a verb.

IN GERMAN

Relative pronouns that are the subject of the relative clause are — 140
in the nominative case. The form depends on the gender and number of the antecedent.

SINGULAR		
MASCULINE	der	
FEMININE	die	*who, that, which*
NEUTER	das	
PLURAL	die	

To choose the correct form,

1. ANTECEDENT — Find the antecedent. (Don't forget that the — 150
   antecedent is always the noun that precedes the relative pronoun.)
2. NUMBER & GENDER — Determine the number and gender of the antecedent.
3. SELECTION — Select the corresponding form in the nominative case.

Here is an example.

> *The man **who visited us** was nice.*
>> 1. ANTECEDENT: man — 160
>> 2. NUMBER & GENDER: **der Mann** *(the man)* is masculine singular
>> 3. SELECTION: masculine singular nominative → **der**

Der Mann, **der uns besuchte**, war nett.

DIRECT OBJECT OF THE RELATIVE CLAUSE
(see *What is an Object?*, p. 55)

IN ENGLISH

There are three relative pronouns that can be used as direct objects of a relative clause, depending on whether the relative pronoun refers to a person or a thing. Since relative pronouns are often omitted when they are objects of a relative clause, we have indicated them in parentheses in the examples below.

Person — *whom* (or *that*) → object of a relative clause
- as a direct object
    This is the student *(whom, that) I saw yesterday.*
- as an indirect object
    Ingrid is the person *to whom* he gave the present.

Thing — *which* or *that* → object of a relative clause
- as a direct object
    This is the book *(which) Axel bought.*
    This is the book *(that) Axel bought.*
- as an indirect object
    Here is the library *to which* he gave the book.

IN GERMAN

Relative pronouns that are the direct objects of the relative clause are either in the accusative or dative case, depending on the verb. The form used depends on the gender and number of the antecedent.

	ACCUSATIVE	DATIVE	
SINGULAR			
MASCULINE	den	dem	
FEMININE	die	der	*who, that, which*
NEUTER	das	dem	
PLURAL	die	denen	

Unlike English, relative pronouns are never omitted in German. (The equivalent English relative pronouns below are in parentheses for reference.)

- as a direct object → accusative or dative
    *Here is the student **(whom, that)** Franz saw last night.*
    Hier ist der Student, **den** Franz gestern Abend sah.
        masc. sing.   masc. sing. acc.

    *The bag **(that)** I'm buying is expensive.*
    Die Tasche, **die** ich kaufe, ist teuer.
      fem. sing.   fem. sing. acc. (**kaufen** takes an accusative object)

*The cat **(that) the dog followed** was black.*
Die Katze, **der** der Hund folgte, war schwarz.

fem. sing. fem. sing. dat. (**folgen** takes a dative object)

INDIRECT OBJECT OR OBJECT OF A PREPOSITION IN A RELATIVE CLAUSE (see p. 57and pp. 64-5 in *What is a Preposition?*)

IN ENGLISH

Relative pronouns used as indirect objects or as objects of a preposition are the same as those used as direct objects. As is the case with other relative pronouns used as objects, they are often omitted. By integrating the preposition "to" before indirect objects and any other preposition within the sentence, you will be able to restore the relative pronoun.

Person — *whom* (or *that*) → indirect object or object of a preposition in a relative clause

*Here is the student **(that) Franz gave the book to**.*

dangling preposition

*Here is the student **to whom** Franz gave the book.*

*Ingrid is the person **(that)** he went out with.*

dangling preposition

*Ingrid is the person **with whom** he went out.*

Thing — *which* or *that* → object of a preposition in a relative clause

*This is the library **that** he was talking **about**.*

dangling preposition

*This is the library **about which** I was talking.*

IN GERMAN

Relative pronouns that are the indirect objects take the dative case. Relative pronouns that are objects of a preposition take the case required by the preposition and reflect the gender of the antecedent. Since German places prepositions directly preceding their objects, you will need to restructure English phrases with dangling prepositions.

*Here is the person **(that) I was waiting for**.* →
*Here is the person **for whom** I was waiting.*
Hier ist die Person, **auf die** ich wartete.

fem. sing. fem. sing. **auf** + acc.

*Here is the person **(that) I was speaking with**.* →
*Here is the person **with whom** I was speaking.*
Hier ist die Person, **mit der** ich sprach.

fem. sing. fem. sing. **mit** + dat.

RELATIVE PRONOUN AS POSSESSIVE MODIFIER

IN ENGLISH

The possessive modifier *whose* does not change its form regardless of its function in the relative clause.

Here are the people *whose* car was stolen.

      | |
antecedent   possessive modifying *car*

Look at the house *whose* roof was fixed.

      | |
antecedent   possessive modifying *roof*

IN GERMAN

The possessive modifier is always in the genitive case. The form used depends on the gender of the antecedent.

GENITIVE			
SINGULAR	MASCULINE	dessen	
	FEMININE	deren	*whose*
	NEUTER	dessen	
PLURAL		deren	

Let's look at an example.

*Hans, **whose alarm clock was broken**, overslept.*

   1. ANTECEDENT: Hans
   2. NUMBER & GENDER: *Hans* is masculine singular.
   3. SELECTION: **dessen**

Hans, **dessen** Wecker kaputt war, hat sich verschlafen.

SUMMARY OF RELATIVE PRONOUNS

Here is a chart you can use as reference.

FUNCTION IN RELATIVE CLAUSE		ANTECEDENT SINGULAR		ANTECEDENT PLURAL
	MASCULINE	FEMININE	NEUTER	
NOMINATIVE	der	die	das	die
ACCUSATIVE	den	die	das	die
DATIVE	dem	der	dem	denen
GENITIVE	dessen	deren	dessen	deren

RELATIVE PRONOUNS WITHOUT ANTECEDENT

There are relative pronouns that refer to an antecedent that has not been expressed or to an entire idea.

IN ENGLISH

The relative pronoun *which* can be used without an antecedent.

She didn't do well, *which* is too bad.

                  |
antecedent an idea: the fact that she didn't do well

IN GERMAN

There is also one relative pronoun that can be used without an antecedent: **was** *(which, what)*.

> Anna hat uns eingeladen, **was** wir nett gefunden haben.
> *Anna invited us, **which we found nice**.*

Your textbook may give you examples of other instances that require the use of **was** as a relative pronoun.

300

STUDY TIPS — RELATIVE PRONOUNS

Pattern

To help you remember the forms of the relative pronouns, look for similarities with another part of speech such as definite articles.

RELATIVE PRONOUNS

	masc.	fem.	neut.	pl.
nom.	der	die	das	die
acc.	den	die	das	die
dat.	dem	der	dem	denen
gen.	dessen	deren	dessen	deren

DEFINITE ARTICLES

	masc.	fem.	neut.	pl.
nom.	der	die	das	die
acc.	den	die	das	die
dat.	dem	der	dem	den
gen.	des	der	des	der

310

What are the similarities between relative pronouns and definite articles?

- nominative, accusative, and dative singular→ identical
- genitive and dative plural → same first 3 letters (**des-, der-, des-, der-**)

Practice

Write two sentences that use the same noun in each sentence. Underline the noun, label its gender, and identify its function (case) in each sentence. Combine the two sentences, replacing one of the nouns with a relative pronoun. Pay attention to the case of the relative pronoun and the verb placement in the relative clause.

320

> **Der Bus** ist spät.   der Bus: masc., subject → nom.
> Ich warte auf **den Bus**.   den Bus: masc., direct object → acc.
> **Der Bus**, <u>auf den ich warte</u>, ist spät.
>
> *The bus is late. I'm waiting **for the bus**. → The bus <u>(that) I'm waiting for</u> is late.*

WHAT IS MEANT BY MOOD?

MOOD in the grammatical sense refers to the forms of a verb that indicate the attitude of the speakers toward what they are saying: are they expressing a fact, a wish, an obligation, giving an order, etc.

Verb forms are divided into moods, which, in turn, are subdivided into one or more tenses. You will learn when to use the various moods as you learn verbs and their tenses. As a beginning student of German, you need to know the names of the moods so that you will understand what your textbook is referring to when it uses these terms.

IN ENGLISH

Verbs can be in one of three moods:

Indicative mood — The indicative mood is used to indicate an action of the verb that really happens or is likely to happen. This is the most common mood, and most of the verb forms that you use in everyday conversation belong to the indicative mood.

> Hans *studies* German.
> Gabi *was* here.
> We *will go*.

The indicative mood has a present tense (see p.54), a past tense (see p. 87), and a future tense (see p. 85).

Imperative mood — The imperative mood is used to express a command. The imperative mood does not have different tenses (see p. 152).

> Hans, *study* German now!
> Anja, *be* here on time!

Subjunctive mood — The subjunctive mood is used to express a subjective attitude or opinion about the action of the verb, a contrary-to-fact statement, or a wish (see p. 154).

> The teacher recommended that Paul *do* the exercise.
> If she *were* here, we would go to the party.
> If only he *were* with us.

IN GERMAN

The same three moods exist and have their own special forms. As in English, the indicative is the most common mood; the imperative is used similarly in both languages; the subjunctive, however, is used much more frequently in German than in English.

40

WHAT IS THE IMPERATIVE?

The IMPERATIVE is a verbal mood used to give someone an order (see *What is Meant by Mood?*, p. 150). Since it does not have different tenses, adverbs of time can be added to indicate when the action should take place (see p. 140).

> *Come* here [now]!
> *Arrive* early tomorrow!

IN ENGLISH

There are two types of commands, depending on who is told to do, or not to do, something.

"You" command — When an order is given to one or more persons, the dictionary form of the verb is used. The command can be softened by adding "please."

> *Answer* the phone.
> *Clean* your room.
>
> *Speak* softly.
> Please *close* the door.

"We" command — When an order is given to oneself as well as to others, the phrase "let's" (a contraction of *let us*) is used + the dictionary form of the verb.

> *Let's leave.*
> *Let's go* to the movies.

The absence of the subject pronoun in the sentence is a good indication that you are dealing with an imperative and not a present tense.

> *You answer* the phone.
>
> present

> *Answer* the phone.
>
> imperative

IN GERMAN

As in English, there are two types of imperatives, depending on who is being told to do or not to do something.

"You" command — The *you*-command has three forms, corresponding to the three different personal pronouns for *you*: familiar **du**, **ihr**, and formal **Sie** (see *What is a Personal Pronoun?*, p. 36). The verb forms of the imperative are the same as the forms of the present tense indicative, except for the **du**-form. In written German an exclamation mark is used after an imperative.

- **du-form** — When an order is given to a person to whom you say **du**, the imperative is formed by using the stem of the verb; some verbs add the ending **-e**.

    Höre!
    Listen.

    Schreib mir bald!
    Write me soon.

- **ihr-form** — When an order is given to two or more persons to whom you say **du** individually, the form of the verb is the same as the present tense indicative.

    Kommt mit!
    Come along.

    Esst nicht so schnell, Kinder!
    Don't eat so fast, children.

As in English, the subject pronoun is usually dropped in the **du** and **ihr** forms.

- **Sie-form** — When an order is given to one or more persons to whom you say **Sie** individually, the subject pronoun **Sie** is placed directly after the **Sie** form of the verb in the present tense. As in English, the command can be softened by adding **bitte** *(please)*.

    Sprechen Sie lauter!
    Speak more loudly.

    Kommen Sie bitte mit!
    Please come along.

"We" command — When an order is given to oneself as well as to others, the subject pronoun **wir** is placed directly after the **wir** form of the verb in the present tense.

    Gehen wir jetzt!
    Let's go now.

    Sprechen wir Deutsch!
    Let's speak German.

Your German textbook will explain in detail the rules for forming the imperative.

CHAPTER

47

WHAT IS THE SUBJUNCTIVE?

The **SUBJUNCTIVE** is a verb mood used to express hypothetical or contrary-to-fact situations, in contrast to the indicative mood that is used to express facts.

> I wish Axel *were* here.
>
> hypothetical (Axel is not here) → subjunctive

> If Axel *were* here, you could meet him.
>
> contrary-to-fact (Axel is not here) → subjunctive

> Axel *is* here.
>
> fact (Axel is here) → indicative

IN ENGLISH

The subjunctive verb form is difficult to recognize because it is spelled like other tenses of the verb, the dictionary form and the simple past tense (see *What is a Verb?*, p. 25 and p. 87 in *What is the Past Tense?*).

INDICATIVE	SUBJUNCTIVE
He *reads* a lot.	The course requires that he *read* a lot.
indicative present *to read*	subjunctive (same as dictionary form)
I *am* in Berlin right now.	I wish I *were* in Berlin.
indicative present *to be*	subjunctive (same as past tense)

The subjunctive occurs most commonly in three kinds of sentences.

- *if-clause* of contrary-to-fact sentences — the subjunctive form of the verb *to be* (*were*) is used. The result clause uses *would* + infinitive. The result clauses are underlined in the examples below.

> If I *were* in Europe now, <u>I would go to Berlin.</u>
>
> subjunctive in *if*-clause [contrary-to-fact: I am *not* in Europe]

> <u>Franz would run faster,</u> if he *were* in shape.
>
> subjunctive in *if*-clause [contrary-to-fact: Franz is *not* in shape]

- conclusion of wish-statements — the subjunctive form of the verb *to be* (*were*) is used. The wish-statement is in the indicative.

> I wish I *were* in Europe right now.
>
> indicative subjunctive

Franz wishes he *were* in shape.

indicative   subjunctive

- following expressions that ask, urge, demand, request, or express necessity — the subjunctive form of any verb is used. ⁴⁰

  She asked that I *come* to see her.

  request   subjunctive same as dictionary form

  It is necessary that he *study* a lot.

  demand   subjunctive same as dictionary form

IN GERMAN

As in English, German has two subjunctive forms: the **SUBJUNC-TIVE II**, so called because the form is based on the second principal part of the verb, i.e., the simple past (see pp. 73-4) is discussed in this chapter. The other, less common subjunctive, the **SUBJUNCTIVE I** (so called because the form is based on the first principal part of the verb, i.e., the infinitive) is discussed in *What is Meant by Direct and Indirect Discourse?*, p. 164. ⁵⁰

The subjunctive II has a present and a past tense formed as follows:

PRESENT SUBJUNCTIVE II — the stem of the indicative past tense, **das Präteritum**, of the verb + subjunctive endings.

- **regular (weak) verbs** — the indicative past and the subjunctive II forms are identical. ⁶⁰

  INFINITIVE: sagen *(to say)*
  INDICATIVE PAST TENSE: sagte *(I said)*
  PAST STEM: sagt-

INDICATIVE PAST	PRESENT SUBJUNCTIVE II
Du **sagtest**...	Wenn du **sagtest**...
Er **sagte**...	Wenn er **sagte**...
You said...	*If you were to say*...
He said...	*If he were to say*...

- **irregular (strong) verbs** — the stem vowels **a, o** and **u** of the indicative past add an umlaut. Note the addition of the letter **-e-** in the subjunctive endings. ⁷⁰

  INFINITIVE: kommen *(to come)*
  INDICATIVE PAST TENSE: kam *(I came)*
  PAST STEM (+ UMLAUT): käm-

INDICATIVE PAST	PRESENT SUBJUNCTIVE II	
ich kam	ich käme	*I came, I would come*
du kamst	du kämest	*you*, etc.
er kam	er käme	
wir kamen	wir kämen	
ihr kamt	ihr kämet	
Sie kamen	Sie kämen	
  ⁸⁰

PAST SUBJUNCTIVE II — the auxiliary verb **haben** *(to have)* or **sein** *(to be)* in the subjunctive II + the past participle of the main verb (see *What is a Participle?*, p. 90).

> Ich **hätte** das Buch **gekauft**, wenn ich es **gefunden hätte**.
> |_____| |_____|
>   past subjunctive   past subjunctive
> *I **would have bought** the book if I **had found** it.*

> Wenn wir nur früher **gekommen wären**!
> |_____|
>   past subjunctive
> *If only we **had come** earlier!*

This tense is often used to talk about things in the past we wish we had done differently.

Consult your textbook for a detailed explanation of the subjunctive II forms, including exceptions.

THE WÜRDE-CONSTRUCTION

In spoken German, and increasingly in written German, the subjunctive II forms of the main verb are often replaced with the present subjunctive II form of **werden** *(to become)* + the infinitive of the main verb, a structure similar to the English structure *would* + the infinitive of the main verb.

ich **würde** kommen	*I would come*
du **würdest** kommen	*you would come*
er, sie, es **würde** kommen	*he, she, it would come*
wir **würden** kommen	*we would come*
ihr **würdet** kommen	*you would come*
sie, Sie **würden** kommen	*they, you would come*

The forms above have the same meaning as the subjunctive II forms: **ich käme, du kämest**, etc.

Let's look at two examples of the **würde**-construction.

> Ich **würde gehen**, wenn ich Zeit hätte.
> *I **would go** if I had time.*

> Sie **würden** dich **einladen**, wenn sie könnten.
> *They **would invite** you if they could.*

USAGE OF THE SUBJUNCTIVE II OR WÜRDE-CONSTRUCTION

The subjunctive II or the **würde**-construction is commonly used in three kinds of sentences.

- *if*-clause and result clause of contrary-to-fact sentences — Unlike English where the verb in the *if*-clause is in the subjunctive and the verb in the result clause uses *would* + infinitive, in German, the subjunctive II or **würde**-construction can be used in either or both clauses.

*If she **were** here, I **would be** happy.*

    subjunctive   *would* + infinitive

Wenn sie hier **wäre**, dann **wäre** ich glücklich.

    subjunctive   subjunctive

*If it **were to rain**, I **would be** sad.*

    subjunctive   *would*
    + infinitive   + infinitive   130

Wenn es **regnen würde**, dann **wäre** ich traurig.

    würde-construction   subjunctive

- both clauses of wish-statements — Unlike English, where the verb in the wish-statement is in the indicative and subjunctive is only used in the conclusion of the wish-statement, in German, the subjunctive II is used in both the wish-statement and in the conclusion.

*I **wish** she **were** here!*

    indicative subjunctive   140

Ich **wünschte**, sie **wäre** doch hier!

    subjunctive   subjunctive

*She **wishes** she **had** more time!*

    indicative   subjunctive

Sie **wünschte**, sie **hätte** mehr Zeit!

    subjunctive   subjunctive

- to form polite requests — Just as English uses the construction *would* or *could* + the infinitive to make polite requests, German uses the verbs **werden** *(to become)* and modals, such as **können** *(to be able to)*, in the subjunctive II + the infinitive.   150

__Could__ you __do__ me a favor?

    could   infinitive

Könntest du mir einen Gefallen **tun**?

    subjunctive   infinitive

__Would__ you please __open__ the door?

    would   infinitive

Würden Sie bitte die Tür **aufmachen**?

    subjunctive   infinitive   160

- the auxiliary verbs **haben** *(to have)*, **sein** *(to be)*, and the modal verbs always use the one-word subjunctive II forms, and not the **würde**-construction (see p. 77 in *What is an Auxiliary Verb?*)

CAREFUL — Pay attention to the use of the umlaut in subjunctive II forms. It not only affects pronunciation, but completely changes the meaning of the sentence. Notice how the umlauted vowel can change the verb tense or mood.

INDICATIVE PAST	SUBJUNCTIVE II
Wir **waren gegangen**.	Wir **wären gegangen**.
*We **had gone**.*	*We **would have gone**.*
Ich **konnte schwimmen**.	Ich **könnte schwimmen**.
*I **was able to swim**.*	*I **would be able to swim**.*

WHAT IS MEANT BY ACTIVE
AND PASSIVE VOICE?

VOICE in the grammatical sense refers to the relationship between   1
the verb and its subject. There are two voices, the ACTIVE VOICE and
the PASSIVE VOICE.

Active voice — A sentence is said to be in the active voice when the
subject is the performer of the action of the verb. In this instance,
the verb is called an ACTIVE VERB.

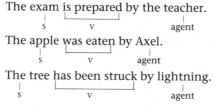

In these examples the subject (S) performs the action of the verb (V)
and the direct object (DO) is the receiver of the action (see *What is a
Subject?,* p. 40 and *What is an Object?,* p. 55).

Passive voice — A sentence is said to be in the passive voice when
the subject receives the action of the verb. In this instance, the
verb is called a PASSIVE VERB.

> The exam is prepared by the teacher.
> | └─┬─┘ |
>   S   V   agent   20
>
> The apple was eaten by Axel.
> | └─┬─┘ |
>   S   V   agent
>
> The tree has been struck by lightning.
> | └──┬──┘ |
>   S   V   agent

In these examples, the subject receives the action of the verb. The
performer of the action, if it is mentioned, is introduced by the
word "by" and is called the AGENT. When the agent is not mentioned, we do not know the performer of the action.

> The lights were already turned on.   30
>> Since there is no agent, we don't know who
>> performed the action of turning on the lights.

IN ENGLISH

The passive voice is expressed by the verb *to be* conjugated in
the appropriate tense + the past participle of the main verb (see
pp. 91-2). The tense of the passive sentence is indicated by the

tense of the verb *to be*. The present passive is usually expressed by the present progressive tense *(is/are being)* rather than the present tense.

40

The exam *is being* prepared by the teacher.
   └────┘
   present

The exam *was* prepared by the teacher.
   │
   past

The exam *will be* prepared by the teacher.
   └──┘
   future

In English, only transitive verbs, i.e., verbs that can have a direct object, can be used in the passive voice.

50

MAKING AN ACTIVE SENTENCE PASSIVE
The steps to change an active sentence into a passive one are as follows.

1. The direct object of the active sentence becomes the subject of the passive sentence.

   ACTIVE   The mechanic repairs *the car.*
                                      │
                                direct object
   PASSIVE   *The car* is repaired by the mechanic.
                  │
               subject

60

2. The tense of the verb of the active sentence is reflected in the tense of the verb *to be* in the passive sentence.

   ACTIVE   The mechanic *repairs* the car.
                              │
                           present
   PASSIVE   The car *is* repaired by the mechanic.
                       │
                    present

   ACTIVE   The mechanic *has repaired* the car.
                            └──────┘
                           present perfect
   PASSIVE   The car *has been* repaired by the mechanic.
                       └──────┘
               present perfect

70

3. The subject of the active sentence becomes the agent of the passive sentence or the agent is omitted.

   ACTIVE   *The mechanic* is repairing the car.
                     │
                  subject
   PASSIVE   The car is being repaired *by the mechanic.*
                                               │
                                            agent

   The car is being repaired. [no agent]

IN GERMAN

The passive voice is formed by the verb **werden** *(to become)*   80
conjugated in the appropriate tense + the past participle of the
main verb.

Der Roman **wird** gelesen.
         |
      present
*The novel **is being** read.*

Der Roman **wurde** gelesen.
         |
     simple past
*The novel **was (being)** read.*

Der Roman **wird** gelesen **werden**.   90
       └——————————┘
          future
*The novel **will be** read.*

Der Roman **ist** gelesen **worden**.
       └——————————┘
        perfect
*The novel **was (has been)** read.*

Der Roman **war** gelesen **worden**.
       └——————————┘
      past perfect
*The novel **had been** read.*

As you can see in the last two examples, in passive sentences   100
the perfect and past perfect tenses drop the **ge-** of the past participle of **werden: geworden → worden**.

MAKING AN ACTIVE SENTENCE PASSIVE

To change an active sentence into passive in German, you can
follow the same steps as for English above. The form of
werden must agree in number with the new subject. The tense
of passive sentence is indicated by the tense of the verb
werden. You will also have to change the case of the words to
reflect their new function in the passive sentence.   110

SUBJECT — The accusative object of an active sentence becomes
the nominative subject of the passive sentence.

    ACTIVE   *The woman reads **the novel**.*
                  Die Frau liest **den Roman**.
                           └————————┘
                            accusative
    PASSIVE   *The novel is read by the woman.*
                  Der Roman wird von der Frau gelesen.
                └————————┘
                 nominative

ACTIVE   *Ilse sings **such songs**.*
Ilse singt **solche Lieder**.
accusative

PASSIVE   ***Such songs** are sung by Ilse.*
Solche Lieder werden von Ilse gesungen.
nominative

AGENT — If the agent is mentioned, it is expressed differently depending on whether it refers to a person or not.

- **person** — If the nominative subject of an active sentence is a person, it is expressed by **von** + dative object in a passive sentence.

ACTIVE   ***Many people** heard the speech.*
Viele Leute hörten die Rede.
nominative

PASSIVE   *The speech was heard **by many people**.*
Die Rede wurde **von vielen Leuten** gehört.
von + dative

- **not a person** — If the nominative subject of an active sentence is not a person, it is usually expressed by **durch** + accusative object in a passive sentence.

ACTIVE   ***Fire** has destroyed the building.*
Feuer hat das Gebäude zerstört.
nominative

PASSIVE   *The building was destroyed **by fire**.*
Das Gebäude ist **durch Feuer** zerstört worden.
durch + accusative

IMPERSONAL PASSIVES

Unlike English where only transitive verbs can be used in the passive voice, German sometimes uses intransitive verbs, verbs that cannot have a direct object, in the passive voice. Such constructions are called **IMPERSONAL PASSIVES** because the verb expresses an activity with no reference to a personal subject. The emphasis is on the activity, rather than on who is doing it. In place of a personal subject, the impersonal pronoun **es** is introduced as the formal subject of the sentence. The auxiliary **werden** is conjugated to agree with **es**.

ACTIVE   Die Angestellten **sprechen** Deutsch.
*The employees **speak** German.*

PASSIVE   **Es wird** hier Deutsch **gesprochen**.
German is spoken here.
[word-for-word: it is here German spoken]

If you change a sentence whose verb takes a dative object from active to passive, the dative object remains in the dative case instead of becoming the subject of the passive sentence. If the impersonal subject **es** is added, the word order has to be changed so that the conjugated verb is in the second position.

ACTIVE   Man dankt i**h**m.

           dative object

           *One thanks **him**.*

PASSIVE   **Ihm** wird gedankt.

           Es wird i**hm** gedankt.   170

           dative subject

           He is thanked.

ACTIVE   Sie glaubten **den Kindern** nicht.

           dative object

           *They didn't believe **the children**.*

PASSIVE   **Den Kindern** wurde nicht geglaubt.

           Es wurde **den Kindern** nicht geglaubt.

           dative subject

           The children were not believed.   180

Note that many impersonal passives in German cannot be translated word-for-word into English. Your textbook will show you several alternatives to the passive construction in German.

CHAPTER

49

WHAT IS MEANT BY DIRECT AND INDIRECT DISCOURSE?

DIRECT DISCOURSE refers to a statement made directly between a speaker and a listener. Direct discourse is usually set in quotation marks.

> Inge said, "I am going to Berlin."
> Axel asked, "What will you do in Berlin?"

INDIRECT (REPORTED) DISCOURSE refers to another person's statement which is reported.

> Inge said she was going to Berlin.
> Axel asked what she would do in Berlin.

While indirect discourse reproduces the substance of the message, it cannot reproduce the statement word-for-word. Some words, such as pronouns and possessive adjectives, must be changed to reflect the change of speaker.

IN ENGLISH

When direct discourse is changed to indirect discourse there is a shift in tense in the reported speech to situate the action in relation to when the speaker reports it.

DIRECT DISCOURSE	Inge said, "*I am going* to Berlin."
	PRONOUNS: I → she
	TENSE: am going (present) → was going (past)
INDIRECT DISCOURSE	Inge said *she was going* to Berlin.
DIRECT DISCOURSE	Inge said, "*I was* in Berlin with *my* sister."
	PRONOUNS: I → she
	POSSESSIVE ADJECTIVE: my → her
	TENSE: was (past) → had been (past perfect)
INDIRECT DISCOURSE	Inge said *she had been* in Berlin with *her* sister.

IN GERMAN

Unlike English where there is only a shift in tense when changing direct to indirect discourse, in German there is also a shift in mood (see *What is Meant by Mood?*, p. 150). In direct discourse the verb is in the indicative, in indirect discourse the verb is in the SUBJUNCTIVE I.

The subjunctive I, so called because it is based on the 1st principal part of the verb, i.e., the infinitive, has a present and a past tense. The same forms are used for weak and strong verbs (see pp. 73-4 in *What are the Principal Parts of a Verb?*).

PRESENT SUBJUNCTIVE I → the stem of the infinitive + the subjunctive endings. The vowel changes in the 1st and 2nd person singular of stem-changing verbs do not apply.

INFINITIVE: fahren *(to drive)*
STEM: fahr-

INDICATIVE PRESENT	PRESENT SUBJUNCTIVE I
ich fahre	ich fahre
du fährst	du fahrest
er fährt	er fahre
wir fahren	wir fahren
ihr fahrt	ihr fahret
Sie fahren	Sie fahren

Here is an example.

DIRECT DISCOURSE Ingrid sagte, "Ich **fahre** nach Berlin."
present indicative
*Ingrid said, "I **am going** to Berlin."*
PRONOUN: I (**ich**) → she (**sie**)
MOOD: I am going (**ich fahre** — indicative) →
she was going (**sie fahre** — subjunctive I)
INDIRECT DISCOURSE Ingrid sagte, sie **fahre** nach Berlin.
subjunctive I present
*Ingrid said she **was going** to Berlin.*

PAST SUBJUNCTIVE I → the subjunctive I form of the helping verb **haben** *(to have)* or **sein** *(to be)* + the past participle of the main verb.

DIRECT DISCOURSE Ingrid sagte, "Ich **war** in Berlin."
simple past indicative
*Ingrid said, "I **was** in Berlin."*
PRONOUN: I (**ich**) → she (**sie**)
MOOD: I was (**ich war** — indicative) →
she had been (**sei gewesen** — subjunctive I)
IINDIRECT DISCOURSE Ingrid sagte, sie **sei** in Berlin **gewesen**.
subjunctive I past
*Ingrid said she **had been** in Berlin.*

The subjunctive I is used primarily in written and news reporting, but is increasingy intermingled with the subjunctive II (see p. 155), which is used in casual conversation. Your German textbook will explain the use of the subjunctive in indirect discourse in greater detail.